D0297852

THE SCOTTISH HIGHLANDERS AND THEIR REGIMENTS

The Scottish Highlanders and their Regiments

by

MICHAEL BRANDER

Seeley, Service & Co. Ltd.

LONDON

First published in Great Britain, 1971
by Seeley, Service and Co. Ltd.
196 Shaftesbury Avenue, London WC2H 8JL

ISBN 0 85422 012 7

PRINTED IN GREAT BRITAIN
BY EBENEZER BAYLIS AND SON LTD.
THE TRINITY PRESS, WORCESTER, AND LONDON

CONTENTS

To

My Kinsman

Lieutenant James Brander

of the

42nd Royal Highland Regiment

The Black Watch

Wounded at Quatre Bras and

Waterloo, June, 1815

ILLUSTRATIONS

Between pages 80 and 81

Between pages 160 and 161

PREFACE

My thanks for their material assistance with this book, as well as for their encouragement, are due to many people, but in particular to Colonel G. A. Rusk, D.S.O., M.C., arbiter of the Black Watch Museum, at Balhousie Castle, Perth, a museum which no visitor to Perth should miss; to Lt. Colonel T. Slessor, at R.H.Q., the Argyll and Sutherland Highlanders, Stirling Castle, another extremely finely situated Regimental Museum; to Major C. R. d'I. Kenworthy at R.H.Q., the Gordon Highlanders in Aberdeen and to Major H. Barker at R.H.Q., the Queen's Own Highlanders, who was responsible for the very fine Regimental Museum in superb surroundings at Fort George; also to Lt. Colonel L. B. Oatts, D.S.O., author of the excellent four volume history of the H.L.I., justly entitled *Proud Heritage*; to Sir Bernard Fergusson, author of several excellent histories of the Black Watch, and Colonel Malcolm of Poltalloch, author of several histories of the Argyll and Sutherland Highlanders, for their encouragement and ready helpfulness; finally to Mr. William Leslie of the County Library, East Lothian and his hard working staff, who along with the staff of the Edinburgh Library put up with my constant demands for more and more background material. The inadequacy of these sketches and the vast omissions involved, of which the author is fully aware, are no fault of theirs, but are due solely to the necessary limitations on length imposed by a very understanding and helpful publisher.

INTRODUCTION

It is astonishing to think that less than 250 years ago there still existed in the Highlands of Scotland a considerable race of hillmen, whose language, customs, arts and even religion had altered little since before the Roman invasion of Britain. Indeed, due to the lack of roads at that time, there was little or no communication with them, and few people who lived south of Perth knew much about them. Since their economy enforced a very simple life and régime, since they wore a garb which, though suited to their hills, was alien to southern eyes, and since, when they did venture from their mountain regions, they invariably carried arms, speaking little or no English, they were thought to be ignorant, savage and dangerous.

The Highlanders differed so completely from the inhabitants of the rest of the British Isles, including the Lowland Scots, that prior to the climacteric of Culloden and for fully fifty years afterwards there was an inherited prejudice against them in the southern mind, based on complete lack of understanding. This was shown clearly in the late 17th century under William III by such Acts of Parliament as those 'for rooting out the Erse language and for other *pious* uses'. Inevitably the rebellions of 1715 and 1745 merely intensified the southern determination to reform the Highlanders in their own image. The Highlanders, on their side, forced to adjust their entire way of life and victims of vicious political and economic pressures, viewed the southerners with bewilderment and a large measure of contempt. The gap was too wide for either to understand the other.

Unfortunately, the mutual distrust of Highlander and Southerner lasted long enough to ensure the economic despoliation of the Highlands, the destruction of the Highland way of life and the dispersion of the Highlanders themselves around the world. Britain's loss was a gain to the developing United States of America, to Canada, to New Zealand and Australia. Yet it was not all loss. In search of an outlet for their natural martial ardour, the Highlanders eagerly joined the Highland regiments, which also offered them a chance to wear the kilt and carry arms, both rights denied them by law for nearly forty years after Culloden. In the Highland regiments the Highlanders shed their blood freely, defending the very culture and economy which had set the seal on their destruction.

Between 1740 and 1815 no less than 86 Highland regiments were embodied. Thousands upon thousands of Highlanders fell in action, in major wars, or small forgotten battles, and as many again died of tropical diseases or the effects of the climate in stations overseas, which were known to decimate the white troops sent to them. While the youth of the Highlands served and died overseas, their parents left behind were driven inexorably from their homeland. The small farmers were replaced by large sheep farms and the Clearances left the straths and glens, which had once supported thriving townships, empty save for the sheep and the Lowland shepherd.

By the mid-19th century the process was complete. The economic pressures from the south had eventually proved too great. The Highlanders were scattered around the world. The glens and straths were deserted except for sheep and deer and the first English tourists. The Highlanders' destruction seemed complete, but they bequeathed in the Highland regiments, in their kilts and tartans, in their clan spirit, their pipe music and their traditional courage and discipline, a final legacy to which the whole of Scotland became proud heir. Here is something of that story up to 1881, when the Cardwell Reforms of the British Army left the Highland Regiments in much the same form as we know them today.

Chapter 1

Formation

On the 3rd of August, 1667 King Charles II issued, under the Great Seal, a commission to the Earl of Atholl to raise and keep such a number of men as he should think fit 'to be a constant guard for securing the peace of the Highlands' and 'to watch upon the braes', his jurisdiction to extend to 'the shyres of Inverness, Nairn, Murray, Banff, Aberdeen, Mairnes, Angus, Perth, Clackmannan, Monteith, Stirling and Dumbarton.' This Highland Watch may thus be regarded as the forerunner of all the subsequent Highland regiments.

In the 17th and for a large part of the 18th century there were no roads penetrating the Highlands and access could only be gained up the glens where the rivers flowed southwards. In those days the glens were well populated and each had its fighting men owing allegiance to their chieftain, great or small: for instance, a thousand Stewarts could be raised in Atholl alone, while Keppoch, only a minor Macdonald chieftain, could call out five hundred men.

The Highland Watch, as the force became known, developed as Independent Companies in increasing numbers towards the end of the 17th century, but in 1717, due largely to the conflicting loyalties resulting from the 'Fifteen' Rising, the Highland Companies were temporarily disbanded by George I. The southerner's suspicion of the Highlanders was displayed in the 'Disarming Acts' which followed the Rising, by which it became an offence for anyone to carry arms openly in the Highlands.

2

This must have proved particularly galling to the Highlander—for he was accustomed to carrying arms always, and using them often. Major-General David Stewart of Garth noted:

> A relation of mine, the late Mr. Stewart of Bohallie, afforded an instance of the Highland character. He was . . . one of the best swordsmen of his time. Latterly he was of a mild disposition, but in his youth had been hot and impetuous and as in those days the country was full of young men equally ready to take fire persons of this description had ample opportunity of proving the temper of their swords and their dexterity in the use of them. Bohallie often spoke of many contests and trials of skill, but they always avoided he said coming to extremities and were in general satisfied when blood was drawn, and 'I had the good fortune never to kill my man.' His swords and targets gave evidence of the service they had seen. On one occasion he was passing from Breadalbane to Loch Lomond through Glenfalloch in company with James Macgregor, one of Rob Roy's sons. As they came to a certain spot Macgregor said: 'It was here that I tried the mettle of one of your kinsmen!' Some miles further on he continued: 'Here I made another of your blood feel the superiority of my sword': 'and here,' said he, when in sight of Ben Lomond, in the country of the Macgregors, 'I made a third of your royal clan yield to the clan Gregor.' My old friend's blood was set in motion by the first remark: the second, as he said, made it boil; however he restrained himself till the third, when he exclaimed: 'You have said and done enough, now stand and defend yourself and see if a fourth defeat of a Stewart will give victory to a Gregarach.' As they were both good swordsmen it was some time before Macgregor received a cut on the sword arm, when, dropping his target, he gave up the contest.

As General Stewart indicated

a Highlander would fight to the last drop of his blood at the command of his Chief, and if he thought his honour, or that of his clan, insulted he was equally ready to call for redress and to seek revenge; yet with this disposition and though generally armed few lives were lost except in general engagements and skirmishes. This is particularly to be remarked in their personal encounters, duels and trials of strength.

No doubt many Highlanders ignored the Disarming Acts, which at that time did not carry the death penalty as after Culloden, although severe enough. General Stewart mentioned 'An old gentleman in Athole, a friend of mine, Mr. Robertson of Auchleeks, carried this spirit so far, that disobeying all restrictions against carrying arms, he never laid them aside, and wore his dirk even when sitting in his dining room, until his death in his 87th year.'

In 1725, at the instigation of the Irish General George Wade, then C-in-C in Scotland, and about to start his epic road-making and fort-building programme, six Independent Companies were raised under Simon, Lord Lovat, Sir Duncan Campbell of Lochnell, Colonel William Grant of Ballindalloch, who held the rank of Captains, and John Campbell of Carrick, Colin Campbell of Skipness and George Munro of Culcairn, who ranked as Lieutenants. These amounted to some five hundred men, raised mostly from clans supposedly loyal to the Hanoverian government. Their objects were to prevent theft and disorder in the Highlands and enforce the Disarming Acts. Whereas the early companies were clothed in their ordinary Highland garb, wearing local, or clan, tartan, General Wade regularized the tartan for all the companies, and from this evolved the dark neutral sett which is now known as 'Black Watch'.

As indicated, the Disarming Acts consequent on the 'Fifteen' were galling to the warlike and spirited Highlanders, and one effect was that they encouraged men of cultured families, many of whom were related to their officers, to join the ranks of the Black Watch simply for the privilege of bearing arms. The result was a hand-picked body of men, fully-trained in the use of arms before being recruited.

These 'gentlemen-soldiers' seem to have been objects of interest to those who saw them. General Stewart recorded:

> The day before the regiment was embodied at Taybridge, five of the soldiers dined and slept in my grandfather's house at Garth. The following morning they rode off in their usual dress, a tartan jacket and truis, ornamented with gold lace embroidery, or twisted gold cords, as was the fashion at the time, while their servants carried their military clothing and arms.

In addition to the Government issue of musket, bayonet, broadsword, cartouche box and belts, they carried a *tuagh* or Lochaber axe, a dirk and a pair of 'dags' or steel pistols, and, in some cases, a *targaid* or shield. These, together with the original, utility, small leather sporran, were furnished privately. Proficiency in handling this formidable armament was proverbial.

General Stewart again quoted his grand-uncle, Mr. Stewart of Bohallie:

> who was one of the gentlemen soldiers in Carrick's company. This gentleman, a man of family and education, was five feet eleven inches in height, remarkable for his personal strength and activity, and one of the best swordsmen of his time, in an age when good swordsmanship was common, and considered an indispensable and graceful accomplishment of a gentleman: and yet, with all these qualifications, he was only centre man of the centre rank of his company.

Captain Burt, an English engineer officer, wrote in a letter to a friend in London:

> I cannot forebear to tell you . . . that many of these private gentlemen-soldiers have gillys, or servants, to attend them in quarters and upon a march, to carry their provisions, baggage and firelocks. (He also noted:) When a son is born to the chief of

a Highland family, there generally arises a contention among the tenants which of them shall have the fostering of the child when it is taken from the nursery. The happy man who succeeds in his suit is ever after called the foster-father; and his children the foster-brothers and sisters of the young laird.

The point Captain Burt seems to have missed is that when a laird's son went away from home he was customarily accompanied by a foster-brother, who would act as bodyguard and servant. When the laird's son joined the army, then naturally the foster-brother joined as well, continuing to act in his capacity as servant whenever the opportunity offered. Indeed, there were many examples of their devotion when they willingly gave their lives in action to save their chief's son.

However, when it came to fighting, the 'gentlemen-soldiers' soon showed they were not lacking in courage, even if, by the standards of the day, their tactics were not entirely orthodox, as the descriptions of their first battle, at Fontenoy in 1745, illustrates clearly enough:

The start was skirmishing work against the French in a wood. This was the kind of operation which was thoroughly understood by the Highlanders, all of whom were great hunters. One of the men left his bonnet hung upon a stick on the edge of a bank to attract the fire of a French sharpshooter, while the Highlander stalked him through the wood and finally shot him. Next morning the Highlanders were selected to accompany a squadron of Austrian Hussars, for they were perfectly able to keep up with the horses for hours on end.

An account of the start of the battle ran as follows:

About four o'clock in the morning the Guards and the Highlanders began the battle and attacked a body of French troops near Vezon. Although their adversaries were stubborn and were entrenched in the village breast high, the Guards with their bayonets and the Highlanders with sword, pistol and dirk forced them out, killing a considerable number. 'Nothing suited the Highlanders more than this sort of fighting. They delighted to run upon the enemy until they came within pistol shot of them, when they discharged their pistols and, running forward, hurled the steelclaw butted weapon at the faces of the foe. Then brandishing their broadswords, they would get to work with them, and those who won within the Highland guard were finished with the dirk.'

General Stewart of Garth recorded:

Lt. Colonel Sir Robert Munro of Foulis, 1st Colonel of the Black Watch, though extremely corpulent, was a most able commander and had obtained leave for the men to fight in their own way. According to the usage of his countrymen he ordered the regiment to clap to the ground on receiving the French fire. Instantly after its discharge the men sprang up and coming close to the enemy poured their shot upon them to the certain destruction of multitudes and drove them precipitately back through their own lines; then retreating, drew up again and attacked a second time after the same manner. These attacks they repeated several times on the same day to the surprise of the whole army. Sir Robert was everywhere with his regiment notwithstanding his great corpulency; and when in the trenches he was hauled out by the legs and arms by his own men. But it was to be observed that when he commanded the whole regiment to clap to the ground, he himself alone stood upright, with the colours behind him, ready to receive the fire of the enemy: and this because, as he said, though he could easily lie down his great bulk would not suffer him to rise so quickly.

Outstanding that day perhaps was the record of Sergeant James Campbell, who killed nine men in succession with his claymore and had his arm blown off by a cannon-ball when he was 'making a stroke at the tenth'. The Duke of Cumberland, who saw this gallant performance himself, applauded his excellent swordsmanship and promised him 'a reward of value equal to an arm'.

The effect of the Black Watch tactics in this first battle may be gauged by the following note by General Stewart:

> A brigade of the Dutch were ordered to attack a rising ground on which were posted the troops called the King of France's Household Guards. The Dutch were to be supported by the Highlanders. The former conducted their march and attack as if they did not know the road—halting and firing every twenty paces. The Highlanders, losing all patience with this kind of fighting, which gave the enemy time and opportunity to fire at their leisure, dashed forward, passed the Dutch, and the front ranks, handing back their firelocks to the rear rank, drew their swords and quickly drove the French from their ground. When the attack was over it was found that of the Highlanders not above a dozen men were killed or wounded, while the Dutch, who had not come up at all, lost more than five times that number.

It was not, however, very long before the British Army and the deadweight of the Establishment in Whitehall began to curb this unorthodox Highland behaviour. First they were to be deprived of their pistols, then their broadswords and finally their dirks. Eventually they were to be armed with musket and bayonet like any other infantry regiments. Their tactics, too, underwent a gradual change. It was not long before they were drilling with the same exactitude as other regiments, and even so were proving themselves capable of adaptability and of holding their own with the best. Their endurance was remarkable. They could march considerable distances at speed and without tiring, and they were generally excellent shots, but in action it was always with the broadsword, or the bayonet, with the charge and with cold steel, that the Highlanders excelled.

They soon made their mark in Europe, and even further afield. Nor is it surprising, considering how little was known of them in Britain in the 18th century, that some remarkably strange ideas about them were current. The French in Guadaloupe in 1759 believed

> that *Les Sauvages d'Ecosse* would neither take nor give quarter, and that they were so nimble that no man could catch them, so nobody could escape them; that no man had a chance against their broadswords and that with a ferocity natural to savages they made no prisoners and spared neither man, woman, nor child.

An article in 'The Vienna Gazette' of 1762 stated authoritatively:

> The Scotch Highlanders are a people totally different in their dress, manners and temper from the other inhabitants of Britain. They are caught in the mountains when young and still run with a surprising degree of swiftness. As they are strangers to fear, they make very good soldiers when disciplined. The men are of low stature, and the most of them old, or very young. They discover an extraordinary submission and love for their officers, who are all young and handsome . . . it is to be hoped that their king's laudable, though late, endeavours to civilise and instruct them in the principles of Christianity will meet with success . . . The French held them at first in great contempt, but they have met with them of late so often, and seen them in the front of so many battles, that they firmly believe that there are twelve battalions of them in the army instead of two.

Chapter 2

Dress

The original uniform of the Highland soldier consisted of the full Highland dress of *breacan an fheilidh*, or plaid and kilt in one, termed in Regimental Orders 'the belted-plaid'. This consisted of twelve yards, or six yards double-width, of tartan, serving as greatcoat, blanket and groundsheet in one, in addition to which the Highlanders were provided with a short jacket, tartan hose and flat blue bonnet. The sporran, or purse, generally of badger skin, which was normal civilian wear, was adopted by the army later.

The full dress was put on in the following manner: the belt was laid down with the plaid over it, the centre of the plaid being over the belt; it was then neatly pleated across the belt, but leaving a part at each end unpleated; the belt was then fastened round the waist, so that the lower half of the plaid formed the *feile*, or kilt, of which the unpleated part became the apron, and the upper half, falling over the belt, formed the *breacan*, or plaid, which was fastened on the left shoulder, or could be thrown round the shoulders like a cloak. By loosening the belt the whole became a blanket, or plaid. (*Plaide* is the Gaelic for blanket.)

It is indicative of the hardiness of the Highlander that, if stranded overnight in the winter when out hunting, it was their custom to soak their plaid in an icy burn, then wring it out until it only contained a little moisture. They then wrapped themselves in it and lay down in the open in the shelter of a gorse bush, or a boulder, the plaid freezing on the outside and thus forming a natural insulation against the weather. Anyone rolling a snowball for a pillow was liable to be considered 'effeminate'.

The belt was the same as that anciently used by the Highlanders, which, according to General Stewart,

> was of strong thick ox leather, and three or four inches in breadth, fixed by a brass or silver buckle in front. When the Highlanders had an expeditious journey to perform, or to run up or down a hill, they tightened the belt, which they said strengthened their loins. They also used the belt for another purpose. When pinched with hunger on their expeditions, they experienced great relief from tightening the belt. This belt was worn by old men within my remembrance (late 18th century) but is now entirely disused in the Highlands (1822).

The full Highland dress was reported as 'looking well on a tall man, but rather like a bundle of clothes on a little man.' It can, however, only be appreciated what freedom the Highlander enjoyed in his traditional dress when comparing it with the normal issue of white breeches for the infantry. According to one who wore these himself:

> they were neither pleasant, cleanly, nor comfortable . . . for the least stain appeared upon them, and the coarse quality of the cloth put washing with pure water and soap out of the question; they had therefore to be rubbed full of pipe-clay and whitening, so as almost to blind the poor man so employed with the dust. Here we had a fair exterior for a field-day; but if the weather was hot, the perspiration and whitening fretted and prickled our thighs; if it rained, the cloth became saturated, the pipe-clay dust was little better than quicklime; if the streets were dirty, the woeful marks flew up from our heels to our breeches as if some wicked elf had followed with a paint brush. But setting aside these serious annoyances, they were generally made so tight and braced up so firm that we almost stood like automata of wood, mechanically arranged for some exhibition on a large scale. To stoop was more than our small-clothes were worth; buttons flying, knees bursting,

back parts rending; and then the long heavy groan when we stood up, just like an old, corpulent, gouty man after stooping to lift his fallen crutch.

Small wonder that the Highlanders in their kilts could outmarch any regiment in the British army. Breeches to the Highlander were a tight purgatory. As late as the early 19th century it was still regarded as a fine joke to introduce a raw Highland recruit to breeches for the first time and persuade him to put them on back to front. The freedom of the kilt was ideally suited to the hills and it is understandable that the Highlanders would readily return to it even after a ban of nearly forty years. It is, of course, questionable how strongly the law was enforced latterly and in the remoter areas at least it was probably flouted without real risk of prison or transportation. Be that as it may, there was general rejoicing when this vicious act was repealed.

A little of just what the kilt meant to the Highlander may be gauged from the following proclamation translated from the Gaelic which was posted throughout the Highlands in 1784 on the repeal of the Act against Highland Dress:

'Listen Men!

This is bringing before all the sons of Gael that the King and Parliament of Britain have for ever abolished the Act against the Highland Dress that come down to the Clans from the beginning of the world to the year 1746. This must bring great joy to every Highland heart. You are no longer bound down to the unmanly dress of the Lowlanders. This is declaring to every man, young and old, simple and gentle, that they may after this put on and wear the trews, the little kilt, the doublet and hose, along with the tartan kilt, without fear of the law of the land, or the spite of enemies.'

The trews, or truis, may best be described as tight tartan trousers with the feet and legs in one piece, worn principally by the chiefs for riding, or journeys. The development of the *philibeg*, or little kilt (worn round the waist in the modern manner without the plaid attached), is attributed by some writers to an Englishman named Parkinson, who is said to have started an iron-works in the Highlands in 1728 and wished to enable his workers to use both arms unhampered by the plaid over one shoulder. Once introduced, it was supposed to have spread with great rapidity. General Stewart commented: 'This opinion is founded on a memorandum left by a gentleman whose name is not mentioned, and published in the *Scots Magazine* . . . it is not worth contradicting.'

Concerning the kilt, he went on to point out:

> The effect of this garb on the Highlanders, even of the present day (1822), is curious. However clownish a young man appears in his pantaloons, walking about with a heavy awkward gait and downcast look, if he dresses in the kilt and bonnet on a Sunday, he assumes a new kind of character, holds his head erect, throws his shoulders back and walks with a strut and mien that might become a Castilian or a Knight of Old Spain.

Suffice it that the dress of the Highland regiments at once presented itself as a challenge to the civil servants in Whitehall. It was soon noted that the kilt required less cloth than the belted-plaid and naturally this was an economy which was insisted on as soon as it was felt tactful to do so. Simply by reducing the amount of cloth issued to each soldier it was easy enough to ensure that this change took place. Other, more subtle, changes followed as the authorities in the south sought to force the Highland regiments to conform with the rest of the British army.

In some respects, the Highlanders themselves set the pace. The Highland bonnet, starting as a flat blue bonnet developed into a tall erection of curling black ostrich feathers with a single hackle at one side. The sporran also underwent a strange metamorphosis from a simple badger skin purse to a tasselled, hairy adornment. Although the bonnet looked both impractical and bulky it proved in practice astonishingly hard wearing and light, cool in summer and warm in winter. It also added to the wearer's height and appearance, and was used more than once to snare a sniper by leaving it on a bush while stalking him from the flank, in the manner indicated in Chapter 1. Yet on many occasions it was the sole piece of clothing to survive a campaign undamaged.

The kilt soon proved itself a suitable garment in all climates. When Fraser's Highlanders landed in North America in 1757 it was suggested that they should wear breeches as it was felt they could not possibly survive the very severe winters and hot summers in the kilt without considerable losses. Both officers and men protested vehemently and thanks to their Colonel's insistence, in the words of a veteran of the campaign:

> We were allowed to wear the garb of our fathers and in the course of six winters showed the doctors that they did not understand our constitutions for in the coldest winters our men were more healthy than those regiments who wore breeches and warm clothing.

General Stewart noted:

> In the march through Holland and Westphalia in 1795 and 1796 when the cold was so intense that brandy froze in bottle, the Highlanders, consisting of the 78th, 79th and the new recruits of the 42nd (very young soldiers) wore their kilts and yet their loss was out of all comparison less than that sustained by some other corps.

One point, however, that the Highlanders suffered, in common with the ordinary British infantry, was the daily drill of hair dressing. This was laid down as follows:

> The hair two inches from the head queued within one inch of the end, of which one inch of hair is to be below the lace of the neck of the coat. The double knot of ribbon to be one inch in length and the single ends to be two inches. It is also wished that the side locks be set back with a little pomatum, as well as that of the forehead, but in no case stiffened with soap.

Sergeant Anton of the Black Watch recorded:

> The tying was a daily penance, and a severe one, to which every man had to submit . . . every morning, daubing the side of his head with dirty grease, soap and flour, until every hair stood like the burr of a thistle, and the back was padded and pulled so that every hair had to keep its due place; and if one less subordinate than the rest chanced to start up in spite of grease, soap-lather and flour, the poor man had to sit down and submit his head to another dressing and afterwards parade for inspection among the defaulters of the regiment . . . it was no uncommon circumstance for us, when on the guard bench asleep, to have the rats and mice scrambling about our heads, eating the filthy stuff with which our hair was debaubed.

Understandably he added thankfully:

> During the time the regiment was quartered in Musselburgh in 1810 a general order was issued for the army to discontinue the tying of hair, and to have it cropped. Never was an order received with more heartfelt satisfaction than this, or obeyed with more alacrity.

Surprisingly enough it was noted that recruits from England and Ireland took to the kilt enthusiastically. The regimental history of the 72nd or Seaforth's Highlanders records in 1802 on their return from India, when they had recruited some 900 young men from the Scots Fencible regiments, that Colonel Macfarlane:

Was now at the head of an efficient body of young men which formed a fine regiment, possessing as true a spirit as any corps. One-fourth of the men and officers were English and Irish, and three-fourths Scotch Highlanders and singular as it may seem, the former were as fond of the kilt and pipes as the latter, and many of them entered completely into the spirit of the national feeling.

In 1804, however, the question of abolishing the kilt seems to have been under active consideration by the military authorities in Whitehall, and a correspondence took place on the subject between the Horse-Guards and Colonel Cameron of the 79th Cameron Highlanders. In a letter headed 'Horse-Guards, 13th October 1804' Colonel Cameron was asked to state his 'private opinion as to the expediency of abolishing the kilt in Highland regiments and substituting in lieu thereof the tartan trews'. Colonel Cameron's characteristically fiery reply, in four involved sentences, ran:

Glasgow, 27th October, 1804.

Sir—On . . . the propriety of an alteration in the mode of clothing Highland regiments . . . I beg to state, freely and fully, my sentiments upon *that* subject, without a particle of prejudice . . . merely founded upon *facts* as applicable to these corps . . . as far as I am *capable*, from thirty years experience, twenty years of which I have been upon *actual* service in all *climates*, with the description of men in question . . . independent of being myself a Highlander and well knowing all the conveniences and inconveniences of our native garb in the field and otherwise, and perhaps, also, aware of the probable source and clashing motives from which the suggestion . . . originally *arose* . . . In the course of the late war several gentlemen proposed to raise Highland regiments . . . adulterated with every description of men, . . . anything but real Highlanders, or even Scotchmen (which is not synonymous) and the colonels themselves being . . . accustomed to wear breeches, consequently *averse* to that free congenial circulation of pure wholesome air (as an exhilarating native bracer) which has hitherto so peculiarly befitted the Highlander for *activity*, and all the other necessary qualities of a soldier, whether for hardship upon scanty fare, *readiness in accoutring*, or making *forced marches &c.*, beside the exclusive advantage, when halted, of drenching his kilt, &c., in the *next brook*, as well as washing his limbs, and drying *both*, as it were, by constant *fanning*, without injury to either, but, on the contrary feeling clean and comfortable, while the buffoon tartan pantaloon &c., . . . sticking wet and dirty to the skin, is not very easily pulled off, and *less so* to get on again in the case of alarm . . . absorbing both wet and dirt, followed up by rheumatism and fevers . . . in hot and cold climates: while it consists with knowledge that the Highlander in his native garb always appeared more cleanly and maintained better health in both climates than those who wore even the thick cloth pantaloons . . . if anything was wanted to aid the rack-renting Highland landlords in destroying that source, which has hitherto proved so fruitful for keeping up Highland corps, it will be that of abolishing their native garb, which His Royal Highness the Commander-in-Chief and the Adjutant General may rest assured will prove a complete death warrant to the recruiting service . . . I sincerely hope His Royal Highness will never acquiesce in so painful and degrading an idea (come from whatever quarter it may) as to strip us of our native garb . . . and *stuff* us into the harlequin tartan pantaloon, which, take away completely the appearance and conceit of a Highland soldier . . . I would rather see him *stuffed* in breeches and abolish the distinction at once—

I have the honour to be &c., (Signed) Alan Cameron.

Colonel 79th or Cameron Highlanders. To Henry Thorpe, Esq.

Colonel Cameron's plea saved the Cameron Highlanders, but on April 7th, 1808 the Adjutant General issued the following memorandum:

As it would be an inducement to the men of the English Militia to extend their services in greater numbers to these

> regiments, it is in consequence most humbly submitted for the approbation of His Majesty, that His Majesty's 72nd, 73rd, 74th, 75th, 91st and 94th Regiments should discontinue to wear in future the dress by which His Majesty's Regiments of Highlanders are distinguished and that the above corps should no longer be considered as on that establishment.

In spite of Whitehall's opposition to the kilt there is no doubt the Highlanders always made a great impression in their full dress both at home and abroad. After Waterloo, an observer in Paris wrote:

> The Highlanders ... are the most martial looking of the military. They attracted the most attention, not only from the French, but from the Allies ... their tartans, bonnets and plumes were much admired ... the fine ladies as they eyed their short kilts through their lorgnettes, confided their fears to each other in whispers: 'My dear, if it should be windy!'

It was, needless to say, a Frenchwoman who first cried: 'Ils sont sans culottes!' Hence, it was as 'Les Sans Culottes' that they were known in France thereafter. This, then, is the answer to those who bring up the eternal question about the Highlander and are not as fortunate as the Czar of Russia after Waterloo. He professed admiration for the Highlanders and a sergeant, a piper and a private from the 42nd, Royal Highland Regiment, from the 79th, or Cameron Highlanders, and from the 92nd, or Gordon Highlanders, were paraded for his private inspection. Sergeant Campbell of the 79th was a man of gigantic stature. According to him: 'The Emperor examined my hose, gaiters, legs and pinched my skin, thinking I wore something under my kilt, and had the curiosity to lift my kilt to my navel so that he might not be deceived.'

On the arrival of the Black Watch in Edinburgh in 1816 Sergeant Anton recorded:

> Our commanding officer's attention was directed towards the thorough equipment of the regiment in what is generally called the Highland costume, part of which had very properly been set aside on our being ordered on actual service . . . Here we were served with plaids, purses and buckles for our shoes . . . The plaid now consists of a yard and a quarter of tartan, a useless shred of cloth, like a child's pinafore reversed and pinned at the back of the shoulder . . . The buckle is for glittering show, not use, for it is merely tied on by the shoe-strings, not as a fastening for the shoe . . . The purse may be considered some decent use, as a sort of apron to keep the kilt properly suspended in front.

A great deal, of course, depended on the commanding officer, but there was a limit to how far even he could go. In 1816, for instance, the 92nd, or Gordon Highlanders, who had just been sent to Jamaica and had already suffered heavy losses from yellow fever, were joined by Colonel Sir Frederick Stovin, an exceedingly obtuse and insensitive, if gallant, Englishman with no qualifications whatsoever for commanding a Highland regiment. He did not attempt to get on with his officers, or listen to their advice. He appeared on parade wearing a cocked hat instead of the Highland bonnet and followed up this insult by issuing orders that the kilt should be replaced by white duck trousers. Word was then passed confidentially to the Duke of York and he was replaced by a Colonel Williamson. The Regimental Record noted: 'The Highland garb, with every part of the original and proper dress of the corps, was immediately resumed.'

By this time, however, the Highlanders were being increasingly brought into line with the other infantry regiments of the British army. In 1819:

> The marching order dress was both cumbersome and heavy, besides taking some time to adjust. The buff pipe-clayed cross-belts carrying the bayonet and ammunition pouches on either side, the heavy knapsack of stiff leather with retaining straps

across the chest, great coat, canteen, water-bottle, haversack and heavy 'Brown Bess' musket, weighing in all some sixty odd pounds required long and constant practice to march in with anything like ease. The tight laced coatee, high leather stock around the neck, and thin low-quartered buckle shoes, which let in all the wet, added further to the discomfort involved.

Another, more succinct, description ran:

> With shoes nick-named 'toe-cases' for all the protection they gave, and buckles, frills, a stock up to the ears, pipe-clayed gloves, about six yards of garters on each leg, muskets with clear locks, often burnished, and well bees-waxed stocks and barrels, they were a singularly equipped set of soldiers.

That well-known Highland regimental historian, A. Mackay Scobie, outlined the end of the story. He instanced a guard mounting in a Highland regiment in 1819 where the officers of the main guard wore full Highland dress, whereas the others, field officer, adjutant and quartermaster, all turned out in the absurd dress of 'white Cashmere pantaloons and short (under the knee) Hessian tasselled boots, and that with a feathered bonnet'. In some Highland regiments there seems to have been a marked reluctance among the officers to wear Highland dress, and their attitude was understandably transmitted to the men, resulting in an outcry against it which was taken up by the Press in 1850.

The entire affair seems to have been the work of a noisy minority, and the actual cause seems to have been the hardness of the tartan supplied by Whitehall at that time. The root of the trouble, if one excepts Whitehall, lay in the fact that the officers of some Highland regiments wore Highland dress so little. Soon after this outburst the officers were ordered to wear the kilt for most duties and this seems to have been generally approved, especially by the younger officers. Thereafter, with the Royal family demonstrating their approval of Highland dress and often wearing it themselves, everyone, Whitehall included, seems to have become reconciled to it and even proud of it. It was only ironic that by this time there were virtually no Highlanders left to wear it.

Chapter 3

Recruiting

The eagerness with which the Highlanders, deprived of the right to bear arms or wear the kilt after the '45, enlisted in the Highland regiments has already been mentioned. This was one potent spur to recruiting. Sheer economic necessity was another, especially towards the end of the 18th century, when many small tenant farmers were evicted to make way for large scale sheep farms in the early 'Clearances'. The choice lay between emigration overseas or a Highland regiment. Many emigrated, but many turned to the recruiting officers. Inevitably, as the Highlanders grew increasingly disenchanted with the broken promises of the authorities in the south, as their economic plight worsened, and as their numbers steadily dwindled, this convenient and seemingly endless source of kilted soldiery available to fight Britain's quarrels overseas, or man her fever-ridden outposts, began to run dry, but one way and another there was little difficulty throughout the latter part of the 18th century in recruiting Highlanders for the Highland regiments.

General Stewart, writing of the 42nd Royal Highland Regiment, or Black Watch, noted:

> In the year 1755 when the establishment of the regiment was augmented preparatory to the war (The Seven Years War with France) the Laird of Mackintosh, then a Captain in the regiment, had charge of all the recruiting parties ... to the Highlands, and quickly collected 500 men, the number he was desired to recruit. Of these he enlisted 87 men in one forenoon.
>
> One morning as he was sitting at breakfast in Inverness, 38

men of the name of Macpherson, from Badenoch, appeared in front of the window, with an offer of their services to Mackintosh: their own immediate chief, the Laird of Cluny, being then in exile, in consequence of his attainder after the Rising. The late General Skinner of the engineers was at breakfast with Mackintosh that morning; and being newly arrived in that part of the country, the whole scene, with all its circumstances, made an impression on his mind, which he never forgot.

The power of a chieftain's name was often enough to raise recruits for a regiment. The Duchess of Gordon offered more. Dressed in regimental jacket and bonnet, she rode round the market-places with her daughters, offering the bounty of a golden guinea and a kiss. Many a gallant Highlander took the kiss and threw the guinea to the onlookers. Small wonder, perhaps, that the Gordon influence proved sufficient to raise four regiments: in 1759 the 89th, or Gordon Highlanders, reduced in 1765 after four years spent in India, during which not a man had been brought to the halberts; in 1778, the 81st, or Aberdeenshire Highlanders, disbanded in 1783; the Gordon Fencibles, embodied in 1793 and disbanded in 1798: finally the 92nd, or Gordon Highlanders, raised in 1794.

Two other instances of the power of a chieftain's name to raise men are worth giving. Lord Macleod, eldest son of the Earl of Cromarty, whose estates were forfeited for his part in the '45, had entered the Swedish Army and attained the rank of Lieutenant-General. In 1777 he returned to England and was favourably received by George III. He was encouraged to try raising a regiment, and so strong was the influence of his name that in a short time he had raised two battalions of the 73rd, or Lord Macleod's Highlanders, in all around 2,200 men, of whom 1,800 were from the neighbourhood in which his family had once possessed power and influence.

The experience of Kenneth Mackenzie, grandson of the Earl of Seaforth, whose estates had also been forfeited, was very similar. In 1771 he bought back the forfeited estates and George III restored his ancient title of Earl of Seaforth. In return, in 1777, he offered to raise a regiment and in 1778 1,130 men were raised as the 78th, or Seaforth's Highlanders. This, immediately after Lord Macleod's battalions had marched south.

Even so, John Macdonald, who enlisted as Pipe Major in the Northern Fencibles raised by the Duke of Gordon in 1778, only needed to spend three months from June to September with Captain Mackay of Bighouse recruiting in Ross-shire. He enlisted on the 4th of June and noted:

> We stayed in the country recruiting till September, and then our party, consisting of 1 captain, 2 lieutenants, 1 ensign, 5 sergeants and 103 privates marched from their different rendezvous to the Meikle Ferry and that night got billets in the town of Tain, where we were very kindly received. The next day we proceeded to Campbelltown near Fort George and from thence to Elgin in Morayshire, which was our headquarters.

Meanwhile, as early as 1762, Admiral Sir John Lockhart, a Lowlander, by taking the surname Ross had inherited the estate of Balnagown in Ross-shire. Retired from the sea, he brought his energies to bear on the problem of 'improving' this inheritance. He started by introducing sheep. Contrary to expectations they throve, and his neighbours soon began to copy his example. That the existing small farm tenants had to be evicted in the process was regarded as incidental, if unfortunate.

In 1791 Sir John Sinclair of Ulbster introduced sheep on his estate in Caithness. Again they proved successful, but Sir John, whose humane intentions were to improve the lot of his small farm tenants, was aghast at the results of his experiment elsewhere. He wrote:

> The first thing that is done is to drive away all the present inhabitants. The next is to introduce a shepherd with a few dogs, and then to cover the mountains with flocks of wild, coarse-wooled and savage animals, which seldom see the shepherd, or are benefitted by his care.

It was too late for regrets. The 'Clearances', begun as a result of the Lowland admiral's first introduction of sheep, now went on remorselessly. As the pace increased, so the scale and brutality of the evictions multiplied. The year 1792 was to have profound repercussions in the Highlands, not least on the recruiting for the Highland regiments. It was the year the Highlanders, driven finally to desperation, tried to halt the woollen tide which threatened to overwhelm them, and learned that the Lowlanders had the law on their side. In Gaelic verse it was remembered ever afterwards as 'The Year of the Sheep'. Like so much to do with the Highlands both farce and tragedy were present, but whereas the farce was purely surface and ephemeral, the tragedy was deep and permanent, unnoticed then, but visible still.

The rebellion of the men of Ross and Sutherland, even if it was short-lived, doomed from the start and achieved nothing, was certainly remarkable for the orderly behaviour of those concerned. Starting from Lairg, the Highlanders, reputedly four hundred strong, marched southwards, forcing the Lowland shepherds who had come north with the sheep to join them in herding the flocks before them. They had nearly reached Alness, some thirty miles south, with around 6,000 sheep, when word came that the Black Watch were on the march from Fort George. The rebels simply faded away in the night, and the soldiers arrived to find the Lowland shepherds and the sheep—nothing more.

Let a young Black Watch subaltern, who was present, describe it in his own words:

> In the autumn the regiment was ordered into Ross-shire on account of some disturbances among the inhabitants, great

numbers of whom had been dispossessed of their farms, in consequence of the new system of converting large tracts of country into pasture . . . A few months after these cold-hearted wholesale ejectments, those who were permitted to remain as cottagers rose in a body and collecting all the sheep which had been placed by the great stock farmers on the possessions which they had formerly held, they drove the whole before them, with the intention of sending them beyond the boundaries of the country; thinking, in their simplicity and despair, that if they got quit of the sheep, they would be again re-instated on their farms . . . no act of violence or outrage occurred; nor did the sheep suffer in the smallest degree . . . (they) did not take a single animal . . . To quell these tumults, which occasioned little less alarm among some gentlemen of Ross than the Rebellion of 1745 the 42nd Regiment were ordered to proceed, by forced marches and the shortest possible route, to Ross-shire.

When they reached the expected scene of action, there was, fortunately, no enemy; for the people had separated and disappeared of their own accord. Fortunate, indeed, it was that the affair was concluded in this manner, as the necessity of turning their arms against their fathers, their brothers, and their friends, must have been in the last degree painful to the feelings of the soldiers and dangerous to their discipline . . .

I was a very young soldier at the time, but on no subsequent occasion were my feelings so powerfully excited as on this . . . Eighteen of the rioters were sent to Inverness for trial. They were eloquently defended by Mr. Charles Ross, advocate, one of their countrymen: but, as their conduct was illegal, and the offence clearly proved, they were found guilty and condemned to be transported to Botany Bay. It would appear, however, that though the legality of the verdict and sentence could not be questioned, they did not carry along with them public opinion, which was probably the cause that the escape of the prisoners was in a manner connived at; for they disappeared out of prison, no-one knew how, and were never enquired after or molested.

With the French Revolution and outbreak of war with France in 1793, the demand for more and yet more Highland soldiers increased. Perhaps typical of recruiting methods at this time was the following:

> A party of the 42nd was recruiting at Paisley during the French Wars, the sergeant in command being a thorough specimen of the true born Highlander. His usual harangue to his gaping audience was as follows:—'Noo then my praw lads, come awa' and 'list in this bauld auld corps—often tried but neffer found wanting—and called the Twa-and Forty Hielandman's Fut and Plack Watches. Commanded by His Royal Grace, Prince Frederick, King o' the Hielands and Emperor o' all the Europes in Scotland. And she'll gie ye the praw dress and the muckle money!'
>
> He would then flourish a bundle of bank notes, which rarely failed to glamour a recruit, on which he would count out his bounty, saying: 'There, my praw lad—sax an twa's ten—awa' wi ye noo, ye damned scoondrel!'

It is not, perhaps, surprising that by the turn of the 18th century the ready supply of recruits from the Highlands was beginning to dry up a little. For all that they were still to be found, one way or another. Alexander Mackay and the Rev. Mr. Sage, Minister of Resolis in Sutherland, both describe the effective methods employed by the Earl of Sutherland. According to Alexander Mackay:

> The method for selecting men in the days of the Earl of Sutherland was for him to call parochial meetings when all the males were formed into regular ranks. The chieftain, or some respectable individual acting for him, with a large snuff box in one hand and an attendant with a bottle of whisky, went along the ranks and to every young man whom he wished to enter the corps, he offered snuff—the signal was perfectly understood—the young man stepped out, took his snuff and dram, and the clerk recorded his name and attestation. They were then collected and the King's Bounty money paid to them until such time as they should be called up for embodiment.

The Rev. Mr. Sage wrote:

> The last event of this period of my life was the raising of the 93rd Highlanders, or Sutherland Regiment, better known under the name '*An Reismeid Catach.*' It was in May 1800 (1799) and Major General Wemyss along with Major Gordon Clunes of Granig and other gentlemen from the coast came up to Kildonan. Their arrival was expected and General Wemyss, to ingratiate himself with the Highlanders sent up to the Manse of Kildonan immense quantities of tobacco twist and strong black rapee snuff, together with the very suitable accompaniment of a large snuff horn, superbly mounted with silver, and having attached to it by a massive silver chain a snuff pen of the same costly material. He was, however, mistaken in the tastes of the Sutherland Highlanders and consequently put himself to unnecessary expense. Smoking was a luxury then utterly unknown and quite unappreciated by the men of Kildonan. What became of the General's supply I know not, but none of it was used, the old men contenting themselves with the snuff their fathers had used before them.
>
> I remember an assemblage on the green to the west of the Manse; it was popularly called 'The Review.' The majority who assembled were tall handsome young fellows, who at the verbal summons of the Countess's ground officer, Donald Bruce, presented themselves before General Wemyss so that he might have for the asking the pick and the choice of them. But while the young men showed no reluctance to enlist, some manoeuvring became necessary to induce their parents to part with them. So two things were promised, first, that the fathers should have the leases of their farms, and next that the sons, if they enlisted, should all be made sergeants. The first promise was to a certain extent fulfilled; the second, it is needless to say, could not possibly be fulfilled.

All in all it was scarcely surprising that recruiting for the Highland regiments began to be more difficult after the turn of the century, or that by 1802 the standard height was lowered to 5 feet 5 inches. The levy money at this time was £6 6s, of which the recruit received in money and necessaries £5 5s; the other payments being—for attesting 1s; surgeon's fee 2/6d; postage and paper 3/6d; reward to party 10/6d and for conducting to a place of approval 3/6d. The recruiting parties were sent to market towns and similar places where young men from the Highlands were likely to be found looking for employment, but the actual enlistment took place at headquarters, hence the last two items.

An example of a recruiting poster of the period 1811–12 reflects the increasing difficulties of recruitment:

The Gallant
Ninety-Second
or Gordon Highlanders

who have so often distinguished themselves at Copenhagen, Spain, on the plains of Holland and the sands of Egypt, and who are now with Lord Wellington in Portugal, want to get a few spirited young men, lads and boys, to whom the greatest encouragement and

Highest Bounty will be given.

From the character of the officers of the regiment who are from this part of the Highlands, they can depend that the interest and advantage of high-spirited and well conducted soldiers from this part of the country will be particularly considered.

Printed at the Journal Office, Inverness.

Progressive disillusionment in the Highlands caused by the broken promises of those in authority, by their own economic plight and by the likely rewards of a military life were all factors adversely affecting recruiting at this time. It was estimated, for instance, that on the extensive Sutherland estates alone between 1811 and 1820 as many as 15,000 people were evicted and forced to find fresh homes, while their old homes were pulled down before their eyes and burned to make way for sheep. Many a wounded Highland soldier returned from the wars 'only in time to find their ancestral dwelling had been swept away and in some cases even in time to see it burning'.

A writer using the pseudonym 'Near Observer' wrote enthusiastically after Waterloo when he had seen the Highland regiments marching past: 'On many a Highland hill and Lowland valley long will the deeds of these men be remembered.' General Stewart commented drily:

> This 'Near Observer' perhaps did not know that, on many a Highland hill, and in many a Highland glen, few are left to mourn the death, or rejoice over the deeds of the departed brave. New views of Highland statistics have changed the birth-place of many a brave soldier and defender of the honour, prosperity and independence of this country, to a desolate waste, where no maimed soldier can now find a home or shelter, and where the sounds of the pipes and the voice of innocent gaity and happiness are no longer heard.

With the end of the war in Europe and disbanding of many of the regiments which had been raised, the immediate crisis in recruiting for the Highland regiments was no longer so acutely obvious. A number of the Highland regiments had already been converted into ordinary infantry regiments, as noted in Chapter 2, and for the moment Whitehall was content to leave matters as they stood. No doubt it occurred to them that at some future date they might need the Highland regiments again.

There were still many Highlanders in the remaining Highland regiments, and even if wealthy Lowland Scots were increasingly taking commissions in these crack regiments there were as yet few Englishmen amongst them. Captain Mackay Chisholm of Glassburn, Strathglass, who joined the 42nd when they were stationed in Malta in 1843, aged sixteen and standing six feet two inches, recorded:

At that period all the officers and men were Scots, almost without exception, and many of them Gaelic speaking Highlanders. Before leaving Malta an Englishman was gazetted ensign in the regiment. His reception was by no means effusive, several of the younger officers, especially, resenting his presence. However the difficulty was eventually overcome. The Englishman was compelled to swallow a Scotch thistle, prickles and all, and to wash it down with a glass of mountain dew. All then shook hands with him as brother Scotsman!

Lieutenant-General Sir John Ewart, who joined the 92nd Gordon Highlanders as a Captain in 1848, wrote:

> The magnificent regiment I was now about to join had always borne a high reputation for discipline and good conduct and was generally considered to be at this time the tallest and finest of any of the line Regiments; it was about the most exclusively national of any of the Highland Corps, about half the men at the time I joined speaking Gaelic.

Two years later Surgeon General William Munro noted as an instance of how different the 93rd were from other Highland regiments that there were: 'So many Highlanders in the ranks who could not speak and did not understand English that the Secretary of State sanctioned 4d per diem as extra pay to 4 corporals to drill the men and explain to them in Gaelic the English words of command.' Little more than a hundred years had passed since Culloden but the 'Erse language' had been nearly rooted out of the Highland regiments. Certainly a great change had taken place in both the Highlands and the Highland regiments.

Indicative of this change was the significant alteration of the nickname for the Highland soldier. The old nickname for the Highland soldier was 'Donald', 'Rory' or 'Her nainsel'. In the latter part of the 19th century this gave way to the essentially Lowland nickname of 'Jock'. This was a word totally unknown in Gaelic and one that had hitherto been reserved only for the Lowland Scottish regiments. The change was, of course, due to the ever growing preponderance of Lowlanders and others in the ranks of the Highland regiments.

On the outbreak of war with Russia in the Crimea, in 1854, the call for recruits once more went forth to the Highlands. There were, naturally, some who responded and the 92nd, or Gordon Highlanders, treasure the story of one young fellow, who was found on being measured not to reach the standard:

'Go home, my lad,' said the Colonel: 'Take more milk to your brose, and come back when you've grown.'

'Oh, sirs,' entreated the lad. 'An' ye'd juist tak me! I'm wee but I'm *wicked*!'

The Colonel could not resist the appeal and an exception was made in his case. But this was an exceptional case in more ways than one. When the second Duke of Sutherland tried to gather volunteers for the Crimean War a different story was told. A meeting was summoned in Golspie and the village was filled with four hundred or more men of Sutherland, who gathered to cheer the Duke politely. He addressed the meeting on the necessity of defeating Russia and the Czar. Beside him on a table as bounty for each recruit sovereigns were piled in a gleaming heap, but no volunteers were forthcoming.

According to Donald MacLeod's '*Gloomy Memories in the Highlands of Scotland*', when the Duke received no reply to his call for volunteers he rose to his feet indignantly and demanded the reason. Eventually one old man moved forward and leaning on his staff addressed him as follows:

> I am sorry for the response your Grace's proposals are meeting here today, so near the spot where your maternal grandmother by giving some forty-eight hours notice marshalled 1,500 men to pick out the 800 she required, but there is a cause for it and a genuine cause and, as your Grace demands to

know it, I must tell you as I see none else is inclined in the assembly to do so. These lands are now devoted to rear dumb animals which your parents considered of far more value than men. I do assure your Grace that it is the prevailing opinion of this county that, should the Czar of Russia take possession of Dunrobin Castle and Stafford House next term that we could not expect worse treatment at his hands than we have experienced at the hands of your family for the past fifty years. Your parents, yourself and your Commissioners have desolated the glens and the straths of Sutherland where you should find hundreds, yea thousands of men to meet and respond to your call cheerfully had your parents kept faith with them. How could your Grace expect to find men where they are not and the few of them that are to be found have more sense than to be decoyed off by chaff to the field of slaughter. But one comfort you have: though you cannot find men to fight, you can supply those who will fight with plenty of mutton, beef and venison.

Chapter 4

Character and Discipline

The Highlander always had a great respect for his pledged word. He regarded his oath as his bond, and his loyalty to clan relationships, or blood ties, was proverbial. He also had a genuine and deep-rooted fear of appearing disgraced before his fellows, either through breaking his word, or through cowardice. His inborn pride was such that he could not face that disgrace. Thus, once the Highlander had taken his oath of allegiance he did not consider it something to be lightly cast aside. Nor, on the other hand, did he expect any promises made to him to be broken. With officers who understood their language and their way of life, this ensured almost perfect discipline. Indeed, cowardice, or lack of discipline, were simply never found in Highland regiments unless ill-officered, or demoralized by outside influences.

In the 18th century most of the officers in Highland regiments were Highland born, and had been brought up and educated in the Highlands. They knew the Highlanders' way of life, their sports and their poetry, and shared a common heritage as well as a common language. The result was an easy familiarity between them based on respect and confidence. An officer of the Black Watch recorded:

> I joined the regiment in 1789, a very young soldier. Colonel Graham, the commanding officer, gave me a steady old soldier, named William Fraser, as my servant—perhaps as my adviser and director. I know not that he had received any directions

on that point, but Colonel Graham himself could not have been more frequent and attentive in his remonstrances, and cautious with regard to my conduct and duty, than my old soldier was, when he thought he had cause to disapprove. These admonitions he always gave me in Gaelic, calling me by my Christian name, with an allusion to the colour of my hair which was fair, or bane, never prefixing Mr. or Ensign, except when he spoke in English. However contrary to the common rules, and however it might surprise those unaccustomed to the manners of the people, to hear a soldier or a servant calling his master simply by his name, my honest old monitor was one of the most respectful, as he was the most faithful, of servants.

The officer himself had necessarily to have similar qualities to the man, only somewhat enhanced. Thus, they must often have appeared outspoken, for in defence of their men's rights they would brook no interference from anyone. A good instance was the attitude taken up by Colonel Cameron of the 79th, or Cameron Highlanders, who raised them in 1793. In 1795 he received the news that it was the intention to draft the Cameron Highlanders into four other regiments. In an interview with the Duke of York, Commander in Chief of the Army he waxed wroth:

To draft the 79th is more than you or your Royal father dare do, he told the Duke of York;

The King, my father, will certainly send the regiment to the West Indies, threatened the Royal Duke.

You may tell the King, your father, from me, retorted Colonel Cameron in a rage: That he may send us to hell if he likes, and I'll go at the head of them, but he *daurna draft us*.

It explains a great deal about relationships with the Highland regiments that the regiment was not drafted but was sent to the West Indies, where it was almost decimated. After two years those who were fit were allowed to volunteer for other corps, and the remainder, under the indomitable Colonel Cameron, returned home.

It was rare for a Lowlander to capture the loyalty of the Highlanders in the same way as a Highlander, but if he was prepared to learn the Gaelic and the Highlander's way of life it could happen. Captain James Baird of Saughtonhall was an officer of the 71st or Fraser's Highlanders, raised in 1775:

> He was not a Highlander, but . . . he studied the character of the people he commanded, he sung their warlike songs, and was frank and familiar as a chief of old, at the same time preserving the full authority of a chief in his character of an officer. He so insinuated himself into their affections that, though Highlanders have a predilection for Highland blood, no chieftain in his glen ever commanded devotion more unreservedly.

When ties of blood, or kinship, were involved the devotion of the Highlander knew no bounds. Captain Fraser of Culduthel, of the Black Watch, was a volunteer at the siege of Bergen-op-Zoom in 1747. He was accompanied by his foster-brother, a common Highland relationship, as his servant. Captain Fraser had joined a night patrol to attack and destroy a battery and had ordered his servant to stay behind:

> The night was pitch dark and the party had such difficulty proceeding that they were forced to halt for a short time. As they moved forward Captain Fraser felt his path impeded, and putting his hand down to discover the cause, he caught hold of a plaid, and seized the owner, who seemed to grovel into the ground. He held the caitiff with one hand and drew his dirk with the other, when he heard the imploring voice of his foster brother.
>
> 'What the devil brought you here?'
>
> 'Just love of you and care of your person.'

'Why so, when your love can do me no good; and why encumber yourself with a plaid?'

'Alas, how could I ever see my mother had you been killed, or wounded, and I had not been there to carry you to the surgeon, or to a Christian burial? and how could I do either without a plaid to wrap you in?'

General Stewart described an incident when the 76th, or Macdonald's, Highlanders were fighting in Virginia under Lord Cornwallis against the Marquis de la Fayette in 1781:

At the moment Lord Cornwallis was giving the order to charge, a Highland soldier rushed forward and placed himself in front of his officer, Lieutenant Simon Macdonald of Morar, afterwards Major in the 92nd Regiment. Lieutenant Macdonald having asked him what brought him there, the soldier replied:

'You know that when I engaged to be a soldier, I promised to be faithful to the King and to you. The French are coming, and while I stand here, neither bullet, nor bayonet, shall touch you, except through my body.'

Major Macdonald had no particular claim to the generous devotion of his trusty follower, further than that which never failed to be binding on the true Highlander—he was born on his officer's estate, where he and his forefathers had been treated with kindness—he was descended from the same family (Clanranald) and when he enlisted he promised to be a faithful soldier.

A remarkable example of the mutual trust between officers and men of the Highland regiments arose when the Breadalbane Fencibles (i.e. Highland Militia) forcibly released two of their number whom they considered wrongly confined to the guard-house. It was pointed out that they were guilty of mutiny and an example must be made, whereupon several men voluntarily offered to stand trial, fully expecting to be condemned and shot. These men were being marched from Glasgow to Edinburgh Castle, when one of them approached the officer in charge with an astonishing proposal.

He explained that

> he knew what his fate would be, but that he had left business of the utmost importance to a friend in Glasgow which he wished to transact before his death: that he himself was fully prepared to meet his fate; but . . . could not die in peace unless the business was settled; and that if the officer would suffer him to return to Glasgow, a few hours there would be sufficient and he would join the party before reaching Edinburgh.

He added:

> You have known me since I was a child; you know my country and my kindred, and you may believe I shall never bring to you any blame by a breach of the promise I now make to be with you in full time to be delivered up in the Castle.

The officer 'was a judicious humane man and knew perfectly his risk and responsibility . . . However, his confidence was such, that he complied with the request of the prisoner.' The man then hurried back to Glasgow, finished his business and left before dawn to rejoin the party. Unfortunately, he was forced to take a circuitous route to avoid being caught as a deserter and failed to arrive at the agreed time and place. The officer was naturally extremely worried, and marched the prisoners as slowly as possible, but eventually,

> unable to delay any longer, he marched up to the Castle, and as he was delivering over the prisoners, but before any report was given in, Macmartin, the absent soldier, rushed in among his fellow-prisoners, all pale with anxiety and fatigue, and breathless with apprehension of the consequences in which his delay might have involved his benefactor.

Countless such instances of the Highlander's steadfastness to his oath could be given, but one other chronicled by General Stewart regarding Macdonald's Highlanders after the siege of Yorktown in 1781, when Lord Cornwallis was forced to surrender, must suffice:

> The 76th was marched in detachments, as prisoners, to different parts of Virginia, where they met with many of their emigrant countrymen, by whom, as well as by the Americans, every endeavour was used and many tempting offers made, to prevail on the soldiers to violate their alliegance, and become subjects of the American government. Yet not a single Highlander allowed himself to be seduced by these offers, from the duty which he had engaged to discharge to his King and country.

A soldier of the 98th, Argyleshire, Highlanders who deserted and emigrated to America, where he settled, found his conscience would not let him rest.

> Several years after his desertion, a letter was received from him, with a sum of money for the purpose of procuring one or two men to supply his place in the regiment, as the only recompense he could make for 'breaking his oath to his God, and his alliegance to his King, which preyed on his conscience in such a manner that he had no rest day or night.'

In 1776, prior to embarking for America to fight the French, who had been encroaching on British territory:

> 3,400 Highlanders of the 42nd and 71st, or Fraser's Highlanders of whom 3,000 were raised and brought from the North in ten weeks, were stationed in Glasgow. The respectable part of the inhabitants were much struck with the regular conduct of these men, so different perhaps from what they had been led to expect. But no part of their conduct was more conspicuous than 'the cordial habits these strangers were in with the people, although so many of them spoke no English;

and more especially their attachment and respect to their officers, and the kindness and familiarity with which the officers talked to the men.

When the regiment (the 71st) was mustered at Glasgow, it was found that more men had come up than were required: these were accordingly left behind when the corps marched to Greenock . . . Several of the men ordered to be left behind . . . followed the regiment, got on board in the dark, and, . . . were not discovered till the fleet was at sea.

Of the Black Watch at this time General Stewart remarked:

The regiment had been now sixteen years embodied and although its original members had by this time almost disappeared, their habits and character were well sustained by their successors . . . The first supply of recruits after their original formation was, in many instances inferior to their predecessors in personal appearance, as well as in private station and family connexions; but they lost nothing of that firm step, erect air, and freedom from awkward restraint, the consequence of a spirit of independence and self-respect, which distinguished their predecessors.

He went on:

There were few courts-martial: and for many years no instance occurred of corporal punishment. If a soldier was brought to the halberts he became degraded, and little more good was expected of him. After being publicly disgraced, he could no longer associate with his comrades; and in several instances the privates of a company have, from their own pay, subscribed to procure the discharge of an obnoxious individual.

Concerning the 78th or Ross-shire Highlanders, raised in 1793, he was even more illuminating:

Among these men desertion was unknown and corporal punishment unnecessary. The detestation and disgrace of such

> a mode of punishment would have rendered a man infamous in his own estimation and an outcast from the society of his country and kindred. Fortunately for these men they were placed under the command of an officer . . . of a family which they were accustomed to respect, and possessing both judgement and temper. He perfectly understood their character and ensured their esteem and regard . . . Colonel Mackenzie knew his men and the value they attached to a good name, by tarnishing which they would bring shame on their country and kindred. In case of any misconduct, he had only to remonstrate, or threaten to transmit to their parents a report of their misbehaviour . . . For several years during which he commanded the regiment, he seldom had occasion to resort to any other restraint. The same system was followed up with such success by his immediate successors.

The threat to report a man to his parents, or to have his name posted in his local parish church, was immensely potent, as it not only entailed disgrace, but ensured that the culprit became an outcast, unable to return to his home. As General Stewart pointed out: 'This was indeed to them a grievous punishment, acting as a perpetual banishment from the country to which they could not return with a bad character.'

The Highlanders at home had their own way of enforcing justice. A case was quoted of a man who was seen apparently quarrelling with a companion in a boat in the centre of Loch Tay. On reaching the shore he claimed that his companion had been drunk and quarrelsome and had fallen overboard and drowned. His story was not believed since he was known as quarrelsome and hot tempered and he was sent to Perth assizes. There he was tried, but acquitted due to lack of evidence. The certainty of his guilt was firmly fixed in everyone's mind.

> On his return to Breadalbane no person would speak to him. He was not upbraided for his supposed guilt, nor was any

attempt made to insult or maltreat him: but he found every back turned upon him and every house he entered instantly emptied of its inhabitants. He withstood this for a short time when he left the country and never returned.

It is easy to understand that the threat of such treatment would be a potent weapon. It is equally easy to imagine the devastating effect of it in the closed society of a regiment or barrack-room, and hence to understand the predicament of any man who transgressed the unwritten code. General Stewart particularly mentions such a case amongst the 78th, or Ross-shire Highlanders:

There were in this battalion nearly 300 men from Lord Seaforth's estate in Lewis. Several years elapsed before any of these men were charged with a crime deserving punishment. In 1799 a man was tried and punished. This so shocked his comrades that he was put out of their society as a degraded man, who brought shame on his kindred. The unfortunate outcast felt his own degradation so much that he became unhappy and desperate; and Colonel Mackenzie, to save him from destruction, applied and got him sent to England, where his disgrace would be unknown and unnoticed. It happened as Colonel Mackenzie had expected, for he quite recovered his character. By the humane consideration of his commander a man was thus saved from that ruin a repetition of severity would have rendered inevitable.

It was undoubtedly difficult for Irishmen or Lowlanders who found themselves unable to fit into the tight Highland pattern, and in the history of the 92nd, Gordon, Highlanders there is a record of the end of two such unfortunates, ostracized by their companions in the Peninsular War because of their bad character. Unable to stand up to the treatment they finally, in desperation, deserted to the enemy.

Some time afterwards one of these men found himself in the front rank of a French Battalion, within hail of the 92nd; for the French, not trusting deserters, employed them in the front, where, not daring to be taken, they were bound to fight. It happened that the regiment had lately been served out with hose tartan: the deserter, in bravado, stuck the piece of red and white cloth, which he still retained, on his bayonet and impudently waved it at his old corps. The Colonel's attention being drawn to it he turned to the men and said:

'Will someone send a pill with my compliments to cure that rascal's impertinence?'

Two crack shots knelt and fired; the 'pill' went home and the deserter's flag was lowered for ever.

In Regimental Orders shortly afterwards the Colonel expressed: 'His mortification at the disgrace attached to the regiment from the desertion of Kelly of the 6th Company and Wellbank of the 2nd Company.' With a certain grim humour he added: 'He does not dread a repetition of so infamous a crime.'

The description of an official 'drumming out' bears repetition:

> A bad character was guilty of a crime so disgraceful to the uniform that but for the guard he would have been lynched by the soldiers. He was sentenced to corporal punishment and to be 'drummed out' . . . After the regimental buttons and facings had been cut from his jacket, a rope was fastened round his neck; with the drums and fifes playing the 'Rogues March' behind he was led by a drummer-boy between the lines of those who had been his comrades, who hissed as he passed to the gate, when a pioneer held out to him his 'ignominious discharge' document in a pair of tongs—and he was no more seen.

Such incidents were clearly very much the exception in the Highland regiments. Writing in 1814 of the behaviour of the 93rd or Sutherland Highlanders, embodied in 1799, it was particularly noted:

The inhabitants of Plymouth were both surprised and gratified at the conduct of the men, who instead of rushing to spend their savings in gin shops and taverns were seen in bookshops supplying themselves with Bibles and such books and tracts as they desired to possess. As at the Cape (where they had been stationed) so they were at Plymouth, steady and sober, while they indulged in dancing and social meetings. Their religious tenets were free of all fanatical gloom and they always promoted that social cheerfulness characteristic of the homes from which they came . . . such of the men as had parents and friends in Sutherland did not forget their condition, in many cases utterly destitute, occasioned by the operation of the 'Clearances' and the so-called improved state of the County. During the short period the Regiment was quartered at Plymouth upwards of £500 was lodged in one banking house to be remitted to Sutherland, exclusive of many sums sent through the Post Office, or by the hands of officers. Some of the sums exceeded £20 from an individual soldier. Men like these did credit to the country of their origin. While spending their money on books the men did not neglect their personal appearance and the haberdasher's shops had their share of trade from the purchase of such extra decorations as the military regulations allowed to be introduced into the uniform.

These were the men who had been enlisted by the Earl of Sutherland's instructions, whose parents in many cases had been promised leases and were now evicted and homeless. Despite the promises which had been made to them and shamelessly broken, they proved to be disciplined soldiers of the first water. In 1815 they were to stand firm in the face of intensive grape-shot and musketry at the siege of New Orleans, and the majority lose their lives or limbs through sheer mismanagement and incompetent orders from above. Those who returned were to find their homes either burned or burning and their parents evicted. Though they might curse the incompetence of the army Generals, or the name of the Duke of Sutherland, they did not blame their officers for these misfortunes.

General Stewart made one very firm point concerning the mixing of non-Highlanders and Highlanders amongst either officers or men. He instanced the 92nd, or Gordon Highlanders, who at that time, around 1816, were undergoing a very low period in their history due to the introduction amongst their ranks, by their recently-appointed and insensitive English Colonel, of several batches of recruits of extremely dissolute character, to make up for heavy losses incurred by yellow fever in Jamaica.

> The old stock of the regiment, who had always maintained the honour and character of the corps, saw themselves debased and contaminated by the comrades introduced into their ranks ... they also saw themselves held in such small consideration by their superiors that any men, however low in character, were considered as fit companions for them ... the force of a bad example prevailed, and in this corps, in which, under more auspicious management and when a purely national regiment, disgraceful punishments were unknown, because unnecessary ... upwards of two hundred have been brought to the halberts in one twelvemonth ... a mixture destroys all ... Unless the ranks be filled by men from the districts whose names are borne by different corps, better far it would be to put an end to the system at once ... I have now to express my fervent hope, that National Corps will either be entirely dissolved and discontinued or preserved pure and unmixed, *both in officers and men.*

One last instance of the feeling between officer and soldier in the Highland regiments is recorded by the Rev. Charles Macdonald, priest of Moidart:

> Many years after the death of Simon Macdonald of Morar, Major in the Gordon Highlanders, a veteran who had served under him was threatened with eviction. He was seen to go to the grave of his old officer, kneel down and conjure him to intervene to prevent injustice to his old follower, emphasizing

his entreaty by striking vigorously with his stick on the green sod of the grave while exclaiming in Gaelic:

'Simon, Simon, you were ever good to me. Come once more to the help of an old comrade and save him from being driven from hearth and home.'

His trust was rewarded. His action was reported to some of the neighbouring gentry and their representations prevailed with the estate agents so that he was allowed to remain.

Chapter 5

Religion and Sobriety

The Highlanders were always notable for their religious tolerance. The effects of the Reformation entirely failed to reach many isolated parts of the Highlands. In other parts three or four chapels would be destroyed and merged into one parish of enormous extent, often without a minister. Itinerant ministers travelled around preaching the gospel, but the overall result was that Roman Catholics, Episcopalians and Presbyterians lived happily cheek by jowl with each other. The continuous bitterness and strife due to religious differences, which plagued the Lowlands throughout the greater part of the 17th century, barely touched the Highlands.

A good example of the reactions of Highlanders to attempts to impose religious change upon them took place at Glenorchy in 1693, when the Episcopalian Minister, the Rev. Mr. David Lindsay, refused to conform and take the oath the Presbyterian government of the Church insisted on:

> Mr. Lindsay was ordered to surrender his charge to a Presbyterian minister then appointed by the Duke of Argyll. When the new clergyman reached the parish to take possession of his living, not an individual would speak to him and every door was shut to him, except Mr. Lindsay's, who received him kindly. On Sunday the new clergyman went to church accompanied by his predecessor. The whole population of the district were assembled, but they would not enter the church. No person spoke to the new minister, nor was there the least noise or violence, till he attempted to enter the church, when he was

surrounded by twelve men fully armed, who told him he must accompany them; and disregarding all Mr. Lindsay's prayers and entreaties, they ordered the piper to play the march of death, and marched the minister to the confines of the parish. Here they made him swear on the Bible that he would never return or disturb Mr. Lindsay. He kept his oath. The synod of Argyle were highly incensed at this violation of their authority; but seeing the people were determined to resist, no further attempt was made, and Mr. Lindsay lived thirty years afterwards and died Episcopal minister of Glenorchy, loved and revered by his flock.

More common, perhaps, was the attitude commented on by Thomas Pennant, the Welsh traveller of the 18th century, in his *Scottish Tour* of 1776 when he visited the Island of Canna:

> The Minister and the Popish priest reside in Eig: but by reason of the turbulent seas that divide these isles, are very seldom able to attend their flocks. I admire the moderation of their congregations, who attend the preaching of either indifferently as they happen to arrive.

In the 17th century, however, William III regarded the strong Jacobite feeling in the Highlands as a threat to his throne. It was with his approval that the Society for the Propagation of Christian Knowledge and the Society for the Reformation of the Highlands were set up, with the avowed aim of spreading the English language throughout the Highlands. Acts of Parliament were passed 'For rooting out the Erse language and for other *pious* uses.' These Acts, together with the fact that, albeit innocently, he had signed the order for the Massacre of Glencoe, combined to make the King's name detested throughout the Highlands. They certainly had the effect of increasing the support for the Jacobites, and may thus have been a contributory factor to the 1715 rebellion.

As a result of these Acts the clergy, itinerant preachers and schoolmasters were all urged to preach and teach in English, which, of course was not understood by the majority of Highlanders. This political bias was intensified after the rebellions of 1715 and 1745. The avowed aim was then not only to rid the Highlands of Highland dress, but also of the Gaelic language, which was henceforth not taught in the schools.

The ministers were appointed by patrons, generally the landowner who owned the parish. Since clergymen were appointed to the Highland parishes who could not speak Gaelic, and since the majority of their parishioners could not speak English some sort of compromise had to be reached. Thus some of the ministers tried to teach themselves Gaelic and preach in that language. General Stewart's comments on this were trenchant:

> If it were proper to be otherwise than serious on such a subject, the appearance the Lowland clergy make in attempting to preach in Gaelic might occasion more than a smile. The mistakes they constantly commit, their perversion of the language and confounding of the meaning of words, which may be understood in two or more senses, occasion ridiculous scenes, which put the gravity of the aged to the proof and throw the young into fits of laughter not easily controlled.

One observer wrote:

> Worthless men were appointed to big parishes by lay patrons quite regardless of their being suitable or unsuitable. This was the case at Gairloch when an old tutor who had hardly a word of Gaelic tried to make up for his want of knowledge by the roaring and bawling he kept up in the pulpit while attempting to read a Gaelic sermon translated from the English by some schoolmaster! ... A small boy, of four or five summers, who had been brought to church for the first time in his life ...

(was) asked . . . what he had seen in the church and his reply was much to the point:

'I saw a man bawling, bawling in a box and no a man would let him oot.'

The situation was an impossible one and resulted, towards the mid-19th century, in the disruption of the Scottish Church, which centred on the right of the congregation to choose their own minister. It was not perhaps as dramatic as the scene at Glenorchy, for it was all extremely orderly. A new minister was presented in 1841 at Marnoch in Aberdeenshire without the congregation's approval. Two thousand people met at the church, and solemnly handed over a resolution intimating that they would withdraw rather than witness his induction. The Rev. Thomas Brown wrote:

The scene that followed was indeed touching and impressive. In a body the parishioners rose, and, gathering up the Bibles, which some of them had been wont to leave for long years from Sabbath to Sabbath in the pews, they silently retired. The deep emotion that prevailed among them was visible in the tears which might be seen trickling down many an old man's cheek and in the flush, more of sorrow than anger, that reddened many a young man's brow . . . No word of disrespect or reproach escaped them . . . They all left.

Fortunately, the standard of chaplains appointed to the Highland regiments was, in general, of a very high standard. The Rev. Dr. Adam Fergusson, afterwards a Professor at Edinburgh University, was the first chaplain of the 42nd Royal Highland Regiment, appointed by Lord John Murray. When he was chaplain it was noted:

He held an equal, if not, in some respects, a greater, influence over the minds of the men than the commanding officer. The succeeding chaplain was Mr. Maclaggan, afterwards Minister at Blair Athole, than who, perhaps, the Highlands of Scotland could not have produced a successor more worthy of Dr. Fergusson, or a chaplain better qualified for a Highland regiment.

There are two accounts of The Rev. Adam Fergusson's behaviour at Fontenoy in 1745, but each indicates that he was indeed a man of spirit. According to one regimental historian:

When the regiment was taking its ground on the morning of the battle, Sir Robert Munro perceived the chaplain in the ranks, and with a friendly caution, told him there was no necessity to expose himself to danger, and that he ought to be out of the line of fire. Dr. Fergusson thanked Sir Robert for his friendly advice, but added that, upon this occasion, he had a duty, which he was imperiously called upon to perform. Accordingly he continued with the regiment during the whole of the action, in the hottest of the fire, praying with the dying, attending to the wounded, and directing them to be carried to a place of safety. By his fearless zeal, his intrepidity, his friendship towards the soldiers (several of whom had been his school-fellows at Dunkeld) and his amiable and cheerful manners; by reproving them with severity when it was necessary, mixing among them with ease and familiarity, and being as ready as any of them with a poem or heroic tale—he acquired an unbounded ascendancy over them.

According to another regimental historian:

Adam Fergusson was advancing into action at the head of the column with a drawn sword in his hand, when Sir Robert Munro saw him and ordered him to the rear with the surgeon. Fergusson refused point blank to go and when the Colonel threatened to have his clergyman's commission cancelled retorted roundly:

'Damn my commission'!

> He then charged at the head of his flock and fought valiantly throughout the bloody fray. Afterwards the stout Munro forgave his insubordination because of his valorous example.

Either way one must agree with General Stewart's conclusion: 'Such chaplains as Dr. Fergusson are rarely to be met with.'

Yet, in fact, the standard seems to have been high. As already noted, Dr. Fergusson's successor seems to have been cast in the same mould and General Stewart particularly notes several other chaplains of Highland regiments, viz: with the 87th and 88th Keith's and Campbell's Highlanders, raised in 1759:

> No trait in the character of these corps was more particularly to be noticed than the respect paid by the men to their chaplain, Mr. Macauley, and the influence which he possessed over their minds and actions. Many of the men, when they got into any little scrape, were more anxious to conceal it from the chaplain than from the commanding officer.

General Stewart, always the Highlander's champion, commented on the activities of evangelical missionaries and others in the Highlands as follows:

> Judging from the establishment of the Society for Propagating Christian Knowledge in the Highlands and others with the same design, and also from the recent reports of missionaries, whose vocation (it may be observed) would fail if they stated that their hearers were pious and intelligent, it may perhaps be believed by many, that previous to these apostolic expeditions and visitations, Christianity must have been little known or practiced in the north. But as the best proof of the existence of religious knowledge and general intelligence is exhibited by the moral character and actions of the people . . . let them speak for themselves.

He then went on to quote the example set by the 93rd or Sutherland Highlanders, when stationed at the Cape of Good Hope from 1805 to 1814:

> Anxious to enjoy the advantages of religious instruction agreeably to the tenets of their national church, and there being no religious service in the garrison, except the customary one of reading prayers to the soldiers on parade, the men of the 93rd regiment formed themselves into a congregation, appointed elders of their own number, engaged and paid a stipend (collected from the soldiers) to a clergyman of the Church of Scotland who had gone out with the intention of preaching to the Caffres (*sic*, Kaffirs) and had Divine Service performed agreeably to the ritual of the established Church. Their expenses were so well regulated that while contributing to the support of their clergyman from the savings of their pay, they were enabled to promote the social cheerfulness which is the true attribute of pure religion and a well spent life. While too many soldiers were ready to indulge in that vice, which, more than any other, leads to crime in the British Army, and spent much of their money on liquor, the Sutherland men indulged in the cheerful amusement of dancing and in their evening meetings were joined by many respectable inhabitants . . . In addition to these expenses the soldiers regularly remitted money to their relations in Sutherland.

Forty years later the 93rd showed that they still maintained this rather striking independence of mind regarding religion. When the disruption of the Church of Scotland took place and the Free Kirk was formed, the bulk of the rank and file of the 93rd, then stationed at Quebec, joined the Free Kirk. The officers, on the other hand, remained with the Auld Kirk. A Dr. Cook was the leading Presbyterian Minister in Quebec and had remained with the Established Church and held special services at that time. The Commanding Officer ordered the 93rd to attend one of these services. The troops were duly marched to Dr. Cook's church and, as was customary, the officers entered first. As soon as they were in, the

Sergeant Major called the Regiment to attention, fell out the Auld Kirk men and marched them into the church. He then marched the remainder to the Free Kirk service, the pipers playing 'It's no my hoose at a' '.

The Commanding Officer is reputed to have taken the Sergeant Major to task later in the day, and demanded to know what he had to say.

'Just this, Sir,' was the answer. 'Both you and I come from a land where we stand no nonsense—the less you say about it the better.' And the Colonel wisely took his advice.

Two anecdotes concerning chaplains in Highland regiments in India bear repetition. In the Kabul campaign of 1879, when the situation looked bad for the Gordon Highlanders, as the cantonment was surrounded, the Rev. Father Brown, the R.C. Padre went round the hospital telling all who could carry a rifle to turn out, saying cheerfully:

'It's Jesus Christ against Mahomet, so we're sure to win.'

On another occasion a private named Jock Shairp was shot in the ankle and, using his rifle as a crutch, hopped back to the shelter of a rock, shouting for a dhooly, or stretcher. The Rev. Mr. Manson, the Presbyterian chaplain, ran up holding out his hands to help him. Thinking he was holding his hands in a position of prayer Jock reassured him:

'Ye've nae need to pray the noo, sir. I'm no gaein' tae dee yet; juist rin an' fetch me a dhooly.'

In general the religious, moral and temperate habits of the Highland regiments were amongst their most noticeable traits, more especially to those accustomed to the behaviour of the normal British infantry regiments. In 1779, when the 42nd, or Royal Highland Regiment, was in its fifth campaign it was noted that the men:

> preserved so completely their original habits of temperance and moderation, that, while rum and all spirituous liquors were served out daily to other troops, the Highlanders received their

allowance every third or fourth day in the same manner as the officers. This was continued until it was found inconvenient for the soldiers to carry more than one day's allowance on long marches . . .

When the 78th, or Ross-shire Highlanders, whose high standards of discipline have already been mentioned, were sent to India in 1795, it was noted:

> The temperate habits of the soldiers and Colonel Mackenzie's mode of punishment by a threat to inform the parents of the misconduct of a delinquent, or to send an unfavourable character of him to his native country, attracted the notice of all India. Their sobriety was such, that it was necessary to restrict them from selling, or giving away, the usual allowance of liquor to other soldiers.

After many years in India it was also recorded that:

> very little change occurred in the behaviour of the men, except that they had become more addicted to liquor than formerly . . . They were steady and economical, lived much among themselves, seldom mixed with other corps, were much attached to many of their officers and extremely national.

It would, of course, be absurd to suggest that all Highland soldiers were always models of sobriety in every circumstance. There were many instances when, misled by the examples of others, or carried away by special circumstances, the Highlanders did give way to temptation. These, it must be noted, however, were almost always when the regiment in question had been fighting abroad for some time, or more often, as Colonel Murray put it, when the Highland blood had been 'adulterated with every description of men'.

A good example of special circumstances was the occasion on August 7th 1795, when the 92nd arrived in Minorca where the 42nd were already. The latter received them with 'the hospitality so characteristic of the Scot abroad. Wine flowed and the quaint old streets of Port Mahon re-echoed with Highland toast and song, and no doubt many a Highland head ached next morning.'

Regimental Orders of the Gordon Highlanders for August 8th read: 'The Lieutenant Colonel will not take any notice of the irregularities which happened last night, on account of the men meeting so many of their friends, but he expects not to have anything more happening of this nature.'

In 1803–4 it was noted regarding the 74th in India:

> Intemperance was an evil habit fostered by the climate and the great facility of indulgence; but it was a point of honour among the men never to indulge when near an enemy, and I often heard it observed that this rule was never known to be broken, even under the protracted conditions of a siege. On such occasions the officers had no trouble with it, the principle being upheld by the men themselves.

At the retreat to Corunna the 92nd, or Gordon Highlanders, were overtaking the troops in front of them and found them destroying a quantity of stores; amongst these was a cask of rum. A young private named Bruce got drunk, fell into the cask and was dead before he could be extricated. At another halt a man, overcome by wine and fatigue, went to sleep too close to the fire and was fearfully burned before his comrades noticed that he had rolled into it. However he was put into the sick cart and 'finally got safe home to Badenoch'.

An interesting Regimental Order appeared in the Gordon Highlander's Orders, dated July 23rd, 1812, during the Peninsular War. It read: 'In future when any officer has occasion to stop the allowance of spirits of any man as a punishment the circumstances are to be always reported to the commanding officer for his concurrence.'

The order was almost certainly occasioned by a story concerning Captain Dugald Campbell, a gallant officer who had risen from the ranks and who had been in every action with the regiment, but who was noted for his thirst and liked to have at least a double allowance of grog. At some bivouacs, however, no liquor was obtainable. Any grog stopped was supposed to be taken to the surgeon, for the use of his patients, but Dugald, no doubt thinking himself as good a judge as the doctor of its disposal, applied it to assuage his own thirst. On one occasion, however, his company was in such good order that he had difficulty in finding any fault, but seizing on a quiet young private he stopped his spirits for having dirty belts. As soon as the parade was dismissed the private marched straight to Colonel Cameron, who, naturally surprised at being thus approached, asked him what he wanted.

'With your leave, sir, I want you to inspect me.'

The Colonel asked what he meant and the young private explained his grievance, pointing out that he did not mind losing his allowance of spirits as much as his character as a clean soldier. 'The Colonel investigated the matter and it was understood that Dugald had a very bad quarter of an hour with his stern chief.'

As noted earlier, by 1840 or thereabouts there were many Lowlanders and others 'adulterating' the Highland regiments. This is perhaps the explanation for the following surprising story, about the hitherto exemplary 93rd, or Sutherland Highlanders. In 1842 they were stationed in barracks at Toronto, several miles outside the city.

> The thirsty souls who liked their grog found it difficult to procure their morning dram. Having made arrangements with a tavern keeper in the city they trained a dog (one of the wise Newfoundland breed) to go to the tavern early every morning with an empty beaker round his neck and money in his mouth and to bring back a supply. The sagacious animal continued

to do this daily for a considerable time, but was at last discovered—caught in the act—and sentenced by the commanding officer to be shot. But the dog was a regimental pet and the regiment in a body petitioned that he might be spared. The request was granted on the condition that he should not be employed again on such degrading work. A promise to this effect was given and honourably kept.

Chapter 6
Mutinies

The mutinies which occurred in various Highland regiments seem today to have a slightly unreal musical comedy atmosphere about them, chiefly because they were generally very orderly mutinies without bloodshed, and due military discipline was usually maintained throughout. They more resembled strikes, which is indeed exactly what they mostly were. In almost every instance they were an attempt by the Highlanders to obtain a settlement of what they believed were their just rights, or to right some wrong they felt had been done to them. The Highlanders had a keen sense of justice as well as a touching faith in authority, and it was only latterly, after repeated betrayals, that they began to lose faith in the authorities in the south or became suspicious of their superiors in the north.

As General Stewart made clear:

> When the Highlanders entered the King's service they considered themselves as a contracting party in the agreements made with the Government, from whom they naturally expected the same punctual performance of their engagements, as well as some degree, at least, of the kindness and attention which they and their fathers had met with from their ancient and hereditary chieftains. When they found . . . the terms which had been expressly stipulated with His Majesty's officers violated, the Highlanders . . . warmly resented such unexpected treatment.

The first and possibly most notorious mutiny of them all was that of the 42nd in 1743. They were ordered to march south to London. The intention was to send them across to Flanders, to join in the War of the Austrian Succession in which Britain had been involved for three years, but the reason they were given was that they were to be inspected by King George I. Many of the 'gentlemen soldiers' felt that they had not enlisted to serve outside the Highlands, and objected to the move on these grounds. Nor were matters improved when it was learned that George I had left England on the day of their arrival in London.

The regiment was reviewed instead by General Wade on May 14th, George I's birthday. Meanwhile, the rumour had been spread, perhaps deliberately by anti-Hanoverian agents, that they were to be sent to the West Indies, then famed as the fever-ridden graveyard of any white soldiers posted there. At that time transportation to the plantations in the West Indies was akin to capital punishment and the Highlanders complained that: 'After being used as rods to scourge their own countrymen, they were to be thrown into the fire.'

By the time the review was over some two hundred of the Highlanders had already made their preparations. Complete with arms and fourteen rounds of ball cartridge apiece, they stole away in the night. Keeping to the country between the two main roads north, they marched by night and lay low by day. Four days later, by which time they had covered almost 100 miles, they were discovered near Oundle and quickly surrounded by dragoons. After some negotiation they agreed to surrender. Thereafter the due machinery of military law took control. They were marched to the Tower and incarcerated.

At this point matters took an unexpected twist. They had behaved with such complete discipline during their march north, neither murdering the sleeping populace in their beds, nor looting unarmed homesteads, as the alarmists had confidently predicted, and they continued to behave with such admirable discipline on their march to the Tower, that public opinion swung round strongly in their favour. Military justice, however, was not prepared to take a lenient view. A hundred and thirty-nine were court-martialled on a charge of mutiny and found guilty. They were condemned to be shot.

From the evidence given at the trial it is obvious that few of them had any real conception of what the entire proceedings were all about. Seventy-nine of them were unable to speak any English and had to rely on an interpreter. Most of the others, inevitably, were unable to follow the legal vernacular involved. Their attitude was more or less summed up by one who stated in evidence: 'I will not be cheated, or do anything by a trick. I will not be transported to the plantations like a thief and a rogue.' Equally obviously, they relied on the defence put forward by another: 'I did not desert. I only wanted to get back to my own country, because they said I would be transported.'

It was obvious that in the circumstances they could hardly shoot them all. In the end three were chosen; a Corporal Samuel Macpherson, who had been one of the leaders, his brother Malcolm, and a Private Farquhar Shaw. They were all tall, handsome, well-built men and they accepted their sentence and marched out to be shot on Tower Hill with a dignity which should have shamed their judges.

A newspaper report read: 'The rest of the Highlanders were drawn up to see the execution . . . The unfortunate men behaved with perfect resolution and propriety.' They were probably more fortunate at that than the remaining hundred and thirty-six, who were drafted to other regiments in fever-ridden outposts such as the West Indies. All those who were punished were regarded by their fellow Highlanders as martyrs to perfidious and treacherous double-dealing by the Government. Suffice it that within four years the Colonel of the Regiment had portraits of the three principals hung in his dining room, which indicates that he considered them at the very most 'misled rather than wilfully culpable'.

As in this instance, almost all the cases of mutiny in the Highland regiments arose because the authorities dealing with the Highlanders imagined that since they spoke little or no English they must be ignorant and unable to understand the nature of the contracts and stipulations they entered into, and hence would be incapable of demanding redress. In practice, if attempts were made to violate their engagements in the terms of the service expected of them or in the pay and allowance promised to them they were likely to become extremely angry. Few things annoyed the Highlander more than a breach of faith. General Stewart summed it up thus:

> Accustomed to yield implicit obedience to their immediate chiefs, who durst not break a compact with a people subject to them . . . and accustomed also to have promises punctually fulfilled, this implicit submission was not yielded when they had rights to be preserved, or agreements to be fulfilled.

A good example of this arose in 1763 when the 87th and 88th, or Keith's and Campbell's Highlanders, who had been raised in 1759, were being reduced after distinguished service in Germany in the War of the Austrian Succession. General Stewart described it thus:

> In the hurry of the campaign new clothing had not been served out to the soldiers for the year 1763, and when they were disbanded, it was thought they had no occasion for military uniforms. The soldiers thought otherwise and said that they were full entitled to pay, clothing and all that had been promised and was therefore due to them. The thing was at first resisted, but the men persevering, it was at length acquiesced in, and an allowance in money given them in lieu of clothing. In this resistance to authority, for the support of what they

considered their rights, some indications of violence, very opposite to their previous exemplary conduct, were manifested. But no disrespect was shown to their officers, nor was any blame imputed to them. On the contrary, the confidence reposed in them by the soldiers remained unshaken.

The next occasion when a mutiny arose in a Highland regiment was in 1778, when the newly raised 78th or Seaforth's Highlanders were marching to Leith from Edinburgh where they were quartered prior to embarking for the East Indies. There they complained that their service engagements had been infringed and that they had pay and bounties due to them. 'About half the regiment, before they had proceeded far, turned back with pipes playing and two plaids fixed on poles instead of colours; they took up a position on Arthur's Seat . . . for several days, during which time the inhabitants of Edinburgh amply supplied them with food.' Fortunately their commander, Major Alexander Donaldson, and the paymaster were able to check the men's complaints and on Lord Macdonald's arrival he advanced the money and, as General Stewart remarked: 'Took the risk of recovering it from those whose conduct had nearly ruined a brave and honourable body of men.'

The claims were all, 'without exception, found to be just. No man was brought to trial, or even put in confinement and when all was settled the Highlanders embarked with the greatest cheerfulness; but, before they sailed, *all the men of Skye and Uist sent their money home to their families and friends.*'

A rather more serious affair occurred in the same year.

In April 1779 two strong detachments of recruits belonging to the 42nd and 71st were ordered from Stirling Castle for the purpose of embarking at Leith to join their regiments in North America. When they arrived at Leith it was notified to them that they were not to join their own regiments but were to be turned over to the 80th and 82nd, the Edinburgh and Hamilton Regiments. The men remonstrated and declared openly their

> firm determination to serve in no corps but that for which they were engaged . . . Troops were sent to Leith, with orders to carry the Highlanders as prisoners to Edinburgh Castle, if they persisted in refusing to be transferred . . . an attempt was made to enforce the orders. The Highlanders flew to arms and a desperate affray ensued. Captain Mansfield of the South Fencible regiment and 9 men were killed and 31 soldiers wounded. At last the mutineers were overpowered and carried to Edinburgh Castle.
>
> On the 6th of May three of these prisoners . . . were brought before a court-martial charged with mutiny in which several of his Majesty's subjects were killed . . .

The first two from the 42nd simply explained as their defence that they had enlisted in the 42nd, their native language was Gaelic and they knew no English. They were always accustomed to the kilt and had never worn trousers, all of which made it necessary for them to serve only in a Highland regiment. The other from Fraser's Highlanders made a similar defence. All stated that at Leith they had been informed that they must now consider themselves in the 82nd or Duke of Hamilton's Lowland Regiment wearing Lowland dress and speaking English, though why, or how, this had happened had not been explained to them. They had maintained they were unfit to serve in this corps and had signified willingness to serve in any other Highland corps, but no regard had been paid to them. They added that they had not received the order to go to Edinburgh Castle, which had they done so they would have obeyed, but had been told in Gaelic they must join the Hamilton Regiment.

For the sake of appearances the three prisoners were found guilty and sentenced to be shot, but they then received a free pardon: 'In full confidence they would endeavour by a prompt obedience and orderly demeanour to atone for this atrocious offence.' The three men afterwards joined the 2nd Battalion of the 42nd, where their character was remarked for steadiness and good conduct. The rest of the detachment also joined the battalion.

In 1783 the 77th or Athole Highlanders, who had been raised in 1778 and stationed thereafter in Ireland, mutinied when an attempt was made to embark them from Portsmouth for India contrary to the terms of service under which they had enlisted. The following account was published in February 1783:

> The Duke of Atholl, his uncle Major-General Murray and Lord George Lennox have been down here but the Athole Highlanders are still determined not to go to the East Indies. They have put their arms and ammunition into one of the magazines and placed a very strong guard over them whilst the rest of the regiment sleep and refresh themselves. They come regularly and quietly to the grand parade, very cleanly dressed, twice a day, their adjutant and officers parading with them. One day it was proposed to turn the great guns on the ramparts on the Highlanders, but this scheme was soon overruled. Another time it was suggested to send for some marching regiments quartered near the place, upon which the Highlanders drew up the drawbridges and placed sentinels at them.

General Stewart noted:

> The regiment was marched to Berwick and disbanded comformably to the original agreement. If Government had offered a small bounty when the Athole Highlanders were required to embark there can be no doubt that they would have obeyed their orders and embarked as cheerfully as they marched into Portsmouth.

He added:

> It is difficult for those not in the habit of mixing with the Highlanders to believe the extent of the mischief which this unhappy misunderstanding has occasioned and the deep and lasting impression it has left behind it . . . always alleged as a

1. The uniform of the Black Watch in 1742

2. A private and an officer of the 79th Cameron Highlanders, 1794

3. The 72nd Duke of Albany's Own Highlanders
by Michael Angelo Hayes

4. The 78th Highlanders, Ross-shire Buffs,
by Michael Angelo Hayes

5. A cartoon entitled 'Souvenirs of the Army of Occupation in Paris, 1815. English uniforms from a French point of view'. The Highlanders are Black Watch

6. A private, colour-sergeant and bandsman of the 93rd Sutherland Highlanders, 1852. Water-colour by R. Poate

7. Uniforms of the 78th Highlanders in India, 1852, by R. Simkin

8. Farquhar Shaw of the 42nd, executed in the Tower, 18 July, 1743, for desertion

9. Sgt James Campbell of the 42nd who slew nine Frenchmen at Fontenoy in 1745, and lost his arm trying to kill a tenth

10. Jean, Duchess of Gordon, raising the 75th Gordon Highlanders in 1794. According to legend, she gave a kiss to each new recruit

confirmation of what happened, at an earlier period, to the Black Watch.

He concluded with the significant point that in spite of the fact that a soldier of the garrison of invalids had been killed and several others wounded in an attempt to prevent the Highlanders from obtaining possession of the main-guard and the garrison parade; 'No man was tried or punished. An inference has in consequence been drawn and never forgotten in the Highlands, that however unjustifiable in the mode of redress, *the men had a just cause of complaint.*'

In 1795 two instances of mutiny occurred in separate Fencible regiments, resulting in an example having to be made in each case. In one instance one man was shot by a firing squad and in the other two men. In each case the reason for the mutiny was that men of the regiment had been confined in the guard room and threatened with corporal punishment. Others of the regiment, in an effort to prevent them being disgraced, had forcibly released them, thus of course making matters far worse. So great was the Highlanders objection to the disgrace involved in corporal punishment that it overcame their sense of discipline.

In the case of the Breadalbane Fencibles, stationed in Glasgow, General Stewart wrote: 'The soldiers being made sensible of the nature of their misconduct and the consequent necessity of a public example (i.e. court-martial and summary execution) *several men voluntarily offered themselves to stand trial.*' They were marched to Edinburgh Castle (one of them, Macmartin, making a remarkable plea to his officer at this point, as already mentioned), where they were court-martialled and four were condemned to be shot. Three were afterwards reprieved, but the fourth, Alexander Sutherland, was shot on Musselburgh Sands.

The mutiny of the Grant Fencibles in 1795 was, in almost every respect, similar to that of the Breadalbane Fencibles. Several men had been confined to the guard room and threatened with corporal punishment. In defiance of their officers the others broke out and released the prisoners. On hearing the news, Sir James Grant, the Colonel of the Regiment, hurried down to Dumfries, where the regiment was then quartered, but he was too late, for the contravention of military order and discipline had been too glaring to be passed over or hushed up. The Regiment was moved north to Musselburgh, where five men were court-martialled and condemned to be shot. One was pardoned, three were allowed to draw lots and one was refused permission to draw. Finally, after this remarkable instance of rough justice, two were shot on Gullane Links on the 16th of July.

The last mutiny in the Highland regiments arose in 1804. Orders had been issued to raise a regiment in the Highlands to be called the Canadian Fencibles and to serve in Canada only. As a result of various circumstances they were speedily recruited. Only that year an entire extensive glen in Inverness-shire, according to General Stewart, had been

> improved in the modern merciless style and depopulated. Several other detached parts of the country had been similarly treated. To the young and active, who had thus lost their homes and their usual mode of subsistence, this corps appeared to present the means of reaching a country where many of their friends and immediate neighbours had gone before them and where they were taught to expect a permanent settlement without being subject to the summary ejectment still practised (1822) in some parts of the north when tenants prove refractory, namely burning their houses about their ears—a mode of ejecting a virtuous peasantry for which the civilised revivers of this obsolete but efficient practice have not received the notice they deserve.
>
> The men of this corps were ordered to assemble in Glasgow, where it was discovered that the most scandalous deceptions had been practised upon them and that terms had been promised which Government would not, and could not,

sanction. The persons who had deceived these poor men by representing the terms in a more favourable light than truth would justify obtained a great number of recruits without any, or for a very small bounty.

When these men discovered their real situation they were loud in their remonstrances, and becoming very disorderly and disobedient were ready to break out into open mutiny. But an immediate enquiry being made into the foundation of their complaints by General Wemyss of Wemyss, who then commanded in Glasgow, they were found to be of such a nature that it was necessary to satisfy them . . . after a full enquiry the whole were discharged . . . numbers of the men enlisted with Colonel Cameron for the 79th and a few (twenty-two) with me for the 78th. Several, who had the money to pay for the passage, emigrated to America. Those who had not the means spread themselves all over the country proclaiming their wrongs, and thus helping to destroy the confidence of their countrymen, not only in Government, but in all public men, whom they now began to think utterly unworthy of credit.

Considering the treatment the Highlanders suffered in the seventy-five years or more after Culloden, refused permission to wear their national dress or carry arms except in the army for very nearly forty years, then evicted from their homes to make way for Lowlanders and sheep, frequently commanded in the army by southerners insensitive to their national feeling and constantly subject to the manipulations of officials in Whitehall, actively opposed to the concept of the Highlands and the Highlanders as something apart or different from the rest of the nation, it is only remarkable that they did not mutiny a great deal more often and a great deal more bloodily. It says much for their remarkable discipline and restraint that they stood as much as they undoubtedly did. Small wonder that by the turn of the 18th century they had already begun to feel that enough was enough.

Chapter 7

Pipes and Pipers

The bagpipes were intended originally to encourage the clans in war, to fire their blood for battle, and inspire them in action. The pipers in a Highland regiment were always regarded in some degree as favoured characters, for there is no doubt that the effects of the pipes on a Highlander could be electrifying. When preparing for battle, or when fatigued, the pipes could affect him in a way nothing else could. His blood would be kindled, his tiredness forgotten and he would be ready for anything.

In the early days of the Highland regiments this was something that the southern mind could not grasp. Indeed, when the 42nd, or Royal Highland Regiment, was fairly newly formed, a determined effort seems to have been made to oust the pipes in favour of the drums, which no doubt the authorities in Whitehall considered a more seemly military instrument. Captain Burt, the English engineer officer, recorded in a letter to his friend in London:

> The Captain of one of the Highland Corps entertained me some time ago at Stirling with an account of a Dispute that happened in one of his Corps about Precedency. The Officer among the rest had received Orders to add a Drum to His Bagpipe as a more military instrument for the Pipe had to be returned because the Highlanders could hardly be brought to march without it. Now, the Contest between the Drummer and the Piper arose about the Post of Honour and at length the Contention grew exceedingly hot, which the Captain having Notice of, he called them both before him, and, in the End,

> decided the matter in Favour of the Drum: whereupon the Piper remonstrated very warmly:
>
> 'Ods wuds, sir,' says he, 'and shall a little Rascal that beats upon a Sheepskin tak' the right hand of me that am a Musician?'

Whatever the result of this particular struggle may have been, the piper soon gained the overall ascendancy. The fact of the matter was that the Highlanders refused to be without their pipes and the pipers came to be accepted as soon as the Highland regiments themselves began to be appreciated for their worth as fighting forces. The pipe major, in particular, became a man of considerable importance in the regiment.

John Macdonald, a schoolmaster in Sutherland, writing his autobiography, recollected:

> About that time (1778) His Grace the Duke of Gordon got a commission to raise a Highland regiment which was to be called the North Fencibles, and Mr. Mackay of Bighouse having a captain's commission in it I was determined to go with him, let the consequence be what it would. So on the 4th of June, 1778 I enlisted with Captain Mackay as pipe-major of the regiment and to have a shilling per day . . . (The) very evening we arrived in Elgin (their headquarters) I was despatched to the Duke of Gordon's house, where I was detained for ten weeks to play the pipes . . . before I left the Duke's house I received two guineas as a present from His Grace for my music.

Transferring later to the 73rd regiment his bounty then was twenty guineas and his pay 1/6d per day, which seems to have been something of an improvement. Whether the Duke of Gordon insisted on his playing in or out of doors at Gordon Castle is a point he does not make clear. General Stewart, however, was very emphatic on this point:

> Playing the bagpipes within doors is a Lowland or English custom. In the Highlands, the piper is always in the open air; and when people wish to dance to his music, it is on the green, if the weather permits; nothing but necessity makes them attempt a pipe dance in the house. The bagpipe was a field instrument intended to call the clans to arms and animate them in battle, and was no more intended for the house than a round of six-pounders. A broad-side from a first-rate, or a round from a battery, has a sublime and impressive effect, at a proper distance. In the same manner, the sound of the bagpipe, softened by distance, had an indescribable effect on the minds and actions of the Highlanders. But as few would choose to be under the muzzle of the guns of a ship of the line, or of a battery, when in full play, so I have seldom seen a Highlander whose ears were not grated when close to pipes, however much his breast might be warmed, and his feelings roused, by the sounds to which he had been accustomed in his youth, when proceeding from the proper distance.

It is understandable enough that those English generals who had not seen the Highlanders in action should be unaware of the effects of the pipes and should look at them askance. Once they had seen the Highlanders in action it was generally unnecessary to emphasize the fact that the pipes had been their inspiration. A very good example of this was seen in the attitude of General Sir Eyre Coote. When the 73rd or Macleod's Highlanders arrived in India he was not impressed by their sickly condition, badly affected both by the voyage and the climate. Indeed he was contemptuous of much about them, referring in particular to the pipes as: 'a useless relic of the barbarous ages ... not in any manner calculated for disciplined troops.'

When it came to the battle of Porto Novo on July 1st 1781, the gallant 73rd, only 500 strong, were the sole British regiment amongst a force of 8,000, opposed to Hyder Ali's forces estimated at: '25 battalions of infantry, 50,000 horse, above 100,000 matchlock men and 47 pieces of cannon, as well as 400 Europeans.' General Sir Eyre Coote, as was his custom, moved around the battlefield. The distinctiveness with which the shrill sounds of the pipes pierced the noise and tumult of the battle and the strong influence they so obviously exercised over the Highlanders completely altered his views on their effectiveness. In particular his attention was attracted by one of the pipers: 'who always blew his most warlike sounds whenever the fire became hotter than ordinary. This greatly pleased the general.'

'Well done my fine fellow,' he cried. 'You shall have a pair of silver pipes for this.'

After the battle was won and Hyder Ali's forces soundly defeated, the General remembered his promise. A very handsome pair of silver mounted pipes were presented to the Regiment. An inscription on them testified to the General's esteem for their conduct and character. This was all the more gratifying in view of his previously sceptical attitude concerning both the Highlanders and their pipes.

The pipes, of course, were not necessarily only played when the Highlanders were going into action, or on the march, and they could sometimes have an unexpected effect on the enemy. It was, perhaps, a pity that General Sir Eyre Coote was not present twelve years later at the siege of Pondicherry when the 72nd, or Seaforth's Highlanders were on trench duty. The Grenadier Company and Captain Gordon's Company of the 72nd were exposed to both the burning August sun and a severe cannonading from the fortress.

Colonel Campbell, the field officer in charge of the trenches, sent his orderly to Lieutenant Campbell of the Grenadier Company to request that their piper might be directed to play some pibrochs. Everyone felt this to be a strange request and somewhat unsuitable in the circumstances, but it was immediately carried out:

> We were a good deal surprised to perceive that the moment the piper began, the fire from the enemy slackened, and soon after almost entirely ceased. The French all got up on the works and seemed more astonished at hearing the bagpipe, than we with Colonel Campbell's request.

The 72nd, or Seaforth's Highlanders, seem to have specialized in piping in unlikely circumstances. When they were at the Cape of Good Hope thirteen years later, in 1806, and had just driven the Dutch from the heights, Captain Campbell noted in his journal:

> The soldiers suffered excessively from the heat of the sun, which was as intense as I ever felt it in India; though our fatigue was extreme, yet, for the momentary halt we made, the grenadier company (72nd) requested the pipers might play them their regimental quick-step, Cabar Feidh, to which they danced a Highland reel, to the utter astonishment of the 59th regiment which was close in our rear.

The pipers in every Highland regiment had a tradition of gallantry in action and any exception to this was at once noticed.

> At the battle of Assaye in India in 1803, the musicians of the Ross-shire Highlanders were ordered to attend to the wounded and carry them to the surgeons in the rear. One of the pipers, believing himself included in this order, laid aside his instrument and assisted the wounded. For this he was afterwards reproached by his comrades. Flutes and hautboys they thought could be well spared, but for the piper, who should always be in the heat of the battle, to go to the rear with the whistlers was a thing altogether unheard of. The unfortunate piper was quite humbled. However, he soon had the opportunity of playing off this stigma, for in the advance at Argaum, he played with such animation and influenced the men to such a degree, that they could hardly be restrained from rushing on

to the charge too soon, and breaking the line. Colonel Adams was, indeed, obliged to silence the musician, who now, in some measure, regained his lost fame.

In 1808 at the battle of Vimeiro in the Peninsular campaign Piper George Clarke of the 71st Highlanders set a particularly high standard. While playing his company forward he was severely wounded in the groin. Although unable to walk and bleeding profusely he propped himself up with his back against a boulder and remarked:

'Deil hae my saul, if ye shall want music!'

He then continued playing a favourite regimental air 'to the great delight of his comrades'.

In recognition of his bravery he was subsequently presented with a set of silver mounted bag-pipes by the Highland Society of London.

No less gallant was Piper MacLaughlan of the 74th at the siege of Badajos in 1812. He was among the first to mount the scaling ladders and as soon as he reached the castle ramparts he began playing the regimental quick step 'The Campbells are Coming', as coolly as if on parade, until his music was abruptly halted by a shot through the bag. He was then seen sitting on a gun carriage with shot flying all around him, calmly repairing the damage. As soon as he had patched the hole, he started playing the stirring air once more, the inspiring sound of his pipes rising high above the tumult of the battle.

At the battle of Vittoria in the following year, 1813, that same Piper MacLaughlan, a great favourite in the regiment, again showed surpassing courage. Major White, then the adjutant, saw the left flank of the regiment charge out of control and wished to recall them:

> The piper, MacLaughlan, seeing I could not collect them, came to my horse's side and played the 'Assembly' on which most of them, who were not shot, collected round me. I was so

> pleased with this act of the piper in coming into danger to save the lives of his comrades and with the good effect of the pipes in the moment of danger, that I told MacLaughlan that I would not fail to mention his gallant and useful conduct.

A moment later the Major was laid low by a musket ball in the shoulder. Then the advance was sounded and MacLaughlan, who was playing behind the colours, was struck by a cannon-ball, which smashed both his legs. In spite of this he demanded to be handed his pipes and went on playing his regiment into battle until he died from loss of blood. When a regimental party went out to bury the dead it was noted as a remarkable circumstance that although the Portuguese peasantry invariably stripped the bodies in the Peninsular battlefields, they had left his body untouched, with his pipes, sword and dirk still beside him as a mark of respect.

The remarkable effect of the pipes on the Highlanders was perhaps never better demonstrated than at the battle of the Pass of Maya in the Peninsular campaign that same year. More than half the men of the 92nd, or Gordon Highlanders, had been killed or wounded and all the officers, except two Lieutenants had been wounded and carried from the field. The 200 soldiers remaining were running short of ammunition and were holding back 3,000 French. It was noted that: 'The advancing enemy were actually stopped by the heaped mass of dead and dying.' 'In all the circumstances' the senior of the two subalterns decided to retire, which they did in perfect order, closely pursued by the French, to the pass, where General Stewart took command.

Pipe Major Cameron, thinking a little music would be welcome to his comrades at this point, set his drones in order and made the hills re-echo with the pibroch 'Dhonuil Dhu'. The effect was electrical. The weary Highlanders were on their legs in an instant, anxiously looking at their wounded General for the order to advance. He at once ordered the piper to stop playing and warned them against the serious consequences of an advance at that particular time.

Meanwhile the French were massing in the pass below and in ten minutes or so the Pipe Major, impatient at his General's waiting tactics, tuned up again, and once more his comrades leaped up eager for action. The General angrily forbade him to play again without orders, on peril of his life. He obeyed, but was heard to mutter in Gaelic: 'If he'll not let me play every man in the land of France will be here soon.'

Reinforcements arrived at last and General Stewart, taking into account the extraordinarily heavy losses and tremendous exertions of the 92nd throughout the day hitherto, ordered them not to join in the charge with the fresh troops. But this time the Pipe Major refused to be silenced. He struck up the charging air of 'The Haughs of Cromdale' and his comrades were instantly seized with a battle frenzy. Without either asking or gaining permission, they not only charged, but led the charge, and rushed down on the French with such irresistible force that they drove them back helter-skelter.

Perhaps typical of battle scenes in the Peninsular campaign was the action of Pipe Major Cameron of the 92nd at the battle of Fuentes d'Onor. While he was playing a particularly inspiring air a bullet ripped the bag of his pipe and resulted in a most appalling piteous squeal as the music died away. Outraged at the insult to himself and his music, and filled with a desire to revenge the damage to his beloved pipes he tied them hastily round his neck and exclaimed loudly in Gaelic:

'We'll give them a different kind of music to dance to now.'

Seizing a musket from a wounded man, he discharged it at the enemy. Then drawing his sword he rushed into the thick of the battle, amid the cheers and laughter of his comrades.

A sergeant of the 2nd Battalion of the 73rd, who conducted many forced marches of over 30 miles a day in Germany in 1813, wrote:

> During our forced marches through Germany the most serviceable man we had was our old piper, Hugh Mackay; who when the men were tired and straggling, would fall back to the rear, and striking up some lively air, he would soon have the whole regiment about him like a cluster of bees. He would often go among the country people playing his pipes to the delight of the inhabitants with whom he was an especial favourite.

True to their traditions of playing their regiment into battle, when the French attacked the 92nd in overwhelming strength at the battle of St. Pierre, two out of the three pipers were killed while playing to encourage their comrades; as one fell another took up the air. In the same way the pipers of the 42nd, or Black Watch, particularly distinguished themselves at Quatre Bras, encouraging their comrades under the heaviest fire and when hard pressed by the French cavalry. In recognition of their gallantry both at Quatre Bras and Waterloo, Sir Denis Pack afterwards presented a set of pipes to the regiment, which were carried by the Pipe Major for many years. It was in such ways that the pipers established themselves as figures of considerable importance in the Highland regiments.

Similar instances of gallantry and inspiration when the pipers played the Highland regiments into action are to be found in every part of the world where they were involved. Sometimes the pipers were men of great courage and coolness. Sometimes they were simply inspired and carried away by their own music. They were usually characters in every sense of the word, gifted with imagination and resource when required. Two examples from the Indian Mutiny of 1857 make this clear.

During the 78th's advance through the streets of Lucknow to relieve the Residency, a piper, who had been fighting his hardest through the mêlée and paying little attention to what had been going on around him, suddenly discovered that he had lost his way in the smoke and the dust and that an enemy cavalryman was riding at him with sword uplifted to cut him down. He had fired his rifle and had no time to fix his bayonet. Instead he seized his bagpipe and blew forth a wild unearthly note which halted the cavalryman's horse as if it had been shot. A moment later it had turned and bolted at a gallop, leaving the piper to find his way safely back to his regiment.

During another engagement a corporal and private of the 78th were carrying a wounded piper back to the rear. They were carrying him on a stretcher when they saw a sepoy on horseback riding furiously towards them with drawn sword. The piper, who was wounded in the leg, raised himself up and after solemnly going through the motions of loading a gun, lifted the longest shank of his bagpipe to his shoulder and aimed it at the sepoy's head. No sooner had he done so than the latter turned rapidly about and galloped away.

Although it was much preferred that the piper should be an outstanding figure of a man, not all pipers were by any means. W. K. Stuart in his '*Reminiscences of a Soldier*' recollected:

> The Colonel of the 86th Regiment had arrived in Antigua (in 1830) bringing with him an Irish piper of the regiment, named O'Kelly, a little elderly man with one leg shorter than the other, an awful drunkard, but a most excellent musician, who could bring from his pipes notes which were deliciously sweet. Of course the Colonel was asked to the Mess of the Highlanders and went, accompanied by his piper. After dinner

> four splendid-looking fellows entered, dressed in full Highland garb, and according to custom, marched round the room, their pipes in full play. Nothing would suit our Colonel, but that O'Kelly should follow their example and perambulate the room. So great was the difference in appearance of the gigantic Highland pipers and the little dot of an Irishman that all were bursting with laughter.

Once it was decided in the south that they wanted Highland regiments there was virtually no way in which the pipes could be excluded. Certainly the attempt to impose the drums on the Highlanders was doomed to failure. As the Highland regiments developed so the pipers themselves developed as an integral part of the regiments. They established a tradition of gallantry in action and a privileged position within the regiment itself, which they have since always maintained. But already, by 1830, the old Highland tradition that the pipes were only meant to be played out of doors had been forgotten, or was ignored. Insidiously the Lowlanders were taking over the Highland regiments from within.

Chapter 8

Ships and Shipwrecks

Since the British live on an island group ships have always been essential in peace and war to transport their troops anywhere else in the world. The Highland regiments were, of course, no different in this respect from any other and it is instructive to note something of the hazards involved before the days of efficient steam-powered vessels. Although it often seems otherwise, it must be assumed that the Highlanders were no more prone to shipwreck than any other troops, unless it is suggested that Whitehall, having failed to kill them off in battle, or by disease, was attempting to drown them instead.

There were other hazards than the weather, as we find from Pipe Major John Macdonald's account of how he joined the 73rd Highlanders in the south, on transferring from the Northern Fencibles. After leaving Fort George he learned of a ship sailing to London:

> So I agreed with her captain for a cabin passage (for which I paid a guinea and a half and was found in victuals and drinks) . . . On the 2nd day of April, 1799, I embarked at Cromarty and the same evening we set sail for London, with a favourable breeze, which increasing soon cleared us of the Firth. We sailed close along the shore after we cleared Peterhead, for fear of French and American privateers that infested the coast at these times.

They met no privateers and the pipe major seems to have enjoyed his journey down the coast:

> Our passage was extremely agreeable, meeting with a great many ships and small craft that traded along the coast. We likewise met several fishing boats who supplied us with fresh fish at a very cheap rate. Off Sunderland we joined a large fleet of colliers bound for different parts of England and kept company with them till we came to Yarmouth Roads, they keeping to sea further than we wanted. After coming through Yarmouth Roads we anchored in a small bay waiting for the tide to carry us to the Nore, to which we proceeded next morning and had a very pleasant prospect of the country on both sides of the Thames, arriving at Hawley's wharf that afternoon after a pleasant voyage of seven days from Cromarty to London.

Of course, privateers apart, such a voyage had few hazards. Navigation was minimal and there were plenty of ports in which to seek refuge in case of emergency. On long sea voyages in troop transports it was often a very different matter, especially on the long journey round the Cape to India, where conditions were sometimes appalling. This was a voyage which could take as much as twelve months and the transports were generally badly provisioned with weevilly ships biscuits and pork preserved in barrels of brine, intensifying a thirst for water scarcely fit to drink. In such circumstances scurvy and other ailments soon attacked even the fittest troops.

On the voyage to India in 1782 the 78th lost 230 men out of 1,100 from scurvy while the 2/42nd, or Black Watch, lost 121 of all ranks from a similar number. Nor were any of them fit to fight for several months after landing. Admittedly this seems to have been a particularly hazardous journey in almost unbelievable conditions even by the standards of the day. Not only were the transports badly provisioned, but the other equipment seems to have been of the sketchiest and the seamen more than usually incompetent.

The officers of the 2/42nd, Black Watch, even found it necessary to take over the navigation:

The *Myrtle*, transport, on board of which were Lieutenant Colonel Macleod and Captains Macdowall and Dalyell, separated from the fleet off the Cape and never afterwards joined. This vessel had neither chart, nor map; and the master being an ignorant seaman, it was owing to Captain Dalyell, who kept a kind of reckoning with deficient instruments, and no maps, but those in Guthrie's geographical grammar—that he made Madagascar, the appointed rendezvous. Seeing no appearance of the fleet, they again sailed and made their way back to St. Helena. Here they procured charts and at length reached Madras on the 23rd of May, 1782.

They were only some three months after the rest of the fleet.

Equally disgraceful was the treatment meted out to the 78th, or Ross-shire Highlanders when they embarked from Guernsey in 1794 to join a military expedition to occupy Zealand. General Stewart recorded:

By an unpardonable neglect, the troops were put on board transports recently arrived from the West Indies with a number of prisoners, of whom many had died of fever in the passage. Without any inspection the same bedding was served out to the troops, who, as might have been anticipated, caught the infection. By great care, it was, however, prevented from spreading.

The 78th seem to have been remarkably unfortunate as far as their sea voyages were concerned. Six companies of the 78th were involved in a full scale shipwreck when sailing from Batavia to Calcutta in the troopship *Frances Charlotte*. They had embarked on the 16th of September, 1816, and had had quite a reasonable voyage until the 5th of November. Then, at two o'clock in the morning, they struck a rock under full sail twelve miles from the small uninhabited island of Prepares.

An account of the behaviour of the troops reads:

> Then was displayed one of those examples of firmness and self-command, which are so necessary in the character of a soldier. Although the ship was in the last extremity and momentarily expected to sink, there was no tumult, no clamorous eagerness to get into the boats: every man waited orders and obeyed them when received.

It seems to have been obvious at once that the ship could not be saved. Inside fifteen minutes it had filled to deck level, but it remained firmly lodged on the rock. The boats were hastily launched and the women, children and sick put aboard them. The only provisions saved, a few bags of rice and some pork, which had been brought up for that day's consumption were also put in the boats which then set off for the island of Prepares. There they had great difficulty in landing due to the rocky shore and heavy surf, so that they were unable to return to the wreck until the following day, the 6th.

Meanwhile those left behind had ferried 140 of their number on a makeshift raft across to a part of the rock which was seen to be exposed at low tide. Once there they lashed themselves on with ropes to prevent the waves which covered it at high tide from washing them off. There they remained with scarcely any food or water for two more days until the boats had ferried everyone from the wreck to the island. Only on the second day, after water had been discovered on the island, did they receive a supply.

The account of the wreck continued:

> During all this time the most perfect order and resignation prevailed, both on the island and on the rock. Providentially the weather continued favourable, or those on the rock must have been swept into the sea. In the evening of the third day, the *Po*, a country ship bound for Penang, appeared in sight, and soon afterwards bore down towards the wreck, of which a small part now only remained above the water. A large boat was immediately sent and forty men taken off the rock.

A smaller boat was then sent, but capsized, and this unaccountably seems to have been too much for the Captain of the *Po*. Without any explanation he simply set sail once again and continued his voyage to Penang, leaving his boat and the wretched survivors on the rock to their fate. Thereupon, not altogether surprisingly, we are informed:

> Several of the men behaved in a most improper manner, and giving themselves up to despair, siezed upon some liquor in the cabin, and threw themselves into a state of intoxication, which added to the wretchedness of their situation. The lascars gave up and could not be made to exert themselves in any way. No part of this misconduct attached to the people on the island, whose conduct was exemplary throughout.

Rescue, fortunately, was at hand. On the morning of the 10th of November Captain Weatherall, commanding the *Prince Blücher*, sighted wreckage floating out at sea and turned towards the island. Sighting the wreck and those remaining on the rock, he lowered boats and took them on board. This was literally in the nick of time, because, although he was able to take the women and children off the island the next morning, a gale then sprang up and had anyone been left on the rock they would certainly have been drowned.

As it was Captain Weatherall lay off the island until the 13th, when, realizing that he had insufficient food for the increased numbers he already had on board, he set sail for Calcutta. He arrived there on the 23rd of November. The Governor-General then promptly sent two vessels with food and clothes to rescue those left on the island. They finally reached Prepares on the 6th of December.

Meanwhile, those left behind on the low, scrub-covered island had almost reached the limit of their endurance. The last of their provisions, a glass full of rice and two ounces of beef every two days for each person, had been eaten and they were reduced to shellfish gathered at low tide. They had neither fishing lines nor fire-arms to kill the monkeys which were the only livestock on the island. Yet it was recorded:

> In this deplorable state the men continued as obedient, and the officers had the same authority as on parade. Every privation was borne in common. Every man who picked up a live shellfish carried it to the general stock, which was safe from the attempts of the half-famished sufferers. Nor was any guard required. However, to prevent temptations, sentinels were placed over the small store. But the precaution was unnecessary. No attempt was made to break the regulations established, and no symptoms of dissatisfaction were shown, except when they saw several ships passing them without notice and without paying regard to their signals.

Yet, after all this, only five men died of weakness, although nine others were drowned, either when ferrying on the makeshift raft between the wreck and the rock, or in the tumultuous surf around the island. In all only fourteen soldiers and two lascars were lost. Considering the various circumstances, this was a remarkable tribute to the discipline and courage of those involved.

As if shipwreck was not bad enough, there was always the additional danger of a fire breaking out in those wooden ships. On March 1st, 1825, while bound for Barbados, the East Indiaman *Kent* caught fire in the Bay of Biscay. Aboard her was Major Duncan MacGregor sailing to join his regiment, the 92nd, with his wife and daughter. When it seemed there was no hope left, Major MacGregor dashed off a last note to his father: 'The ship, *Kent*, Indiaman, is on fire, Elizabeth, Joanna and myself commit our spirits into the hands of our blessed Redeemer. His Grace enables us to be quite composed in the awful prospect of entering eternity.' He then sealed it in a bottle and tossed it into the sea.

Fortunately for all concerned, at the last possible moment a small brig, the *Cambria*, sighted the fire and managed to save most of those on board, although some were killed when the *Kent* blew up. The bottle itself was picked up in the Barbados on the 30th of September 1826. When Major MacGregor eventually joined the 93rd in February 1827 the letter was given to him by the finder.

In 1826 Barbados was also the scene of the wreck of the Admiralty transport *Shipley*, with fresh drafts for several Highland regiments under command of Lieutenant George Drummond of the 93rd. The man on watch went to sleep and she was wrecked on a dark April night on the Cobbler's Rocks at the east point of Barbados. Fortunately, the boatswain managed to cast a line ashore to the cliff top, and a breeches buoy was rigged up. The women and children and then the remainder were all hauled to safety. Finally Lieutenant Drummond himself left the ship, which soon afterwards broke up with the loss of some 130 tons of stores, but no lives.

Perhaps the most famous shipwreck of them all, however, was that of the iron paddle-driven troopship *Birkenhead* of 1,400 tons and 556 horsepower, commanded by Master Commander Robert Salmond. It was not really such an epic tale of adventure as the wreck of the *Frances Charlotte*, but it received much greater publicity and the behaviour of the troops was certainly of a similar high standard. There were several other features in common between the two occasions, but the loss of life, much of it perhaps unnecessary, was far greater in the case of the *Birkenhead*. This was possibly another feature which caught the imagination of a world still unaccustomed to reading of multiple deaths in everyday travel.

The *Birkenhead* sailed from Cork for the Cape of Good Hope in early January 1852, with detachments from the depots of ten regiments all under the command of Lieutenant Colonel Seton of the 74th Highlanders. On board, including the crew of 132, were 631 people, many of them the wives and children of the soldiers. They had a fair passage out to the Cape and arrived at Simon's Bay on the 23rd of February, when Captain Salmond was ordered to land the troops at Algoa Bay.

The ship left Simon's Bay on the evening of the 25th with a calm sea and a clear starlit night. A look-out was posted and a leadsman stationed at the port paddle-box nearest the land which was about three miles away. In spite of these precautions the *Birkenhead* suddenly struck on a jagged, sunken rock at about 2 a.m. on the morning of the 26th. Many of the soldiers sleeping in the forepart of the ship were drowned instantly as water flooded in on them.

Captain Salmond at once appeared on deck and ordered the engine to be stopped, the bower anchor to be let go, the paddle-box boats to be got out and the quarter-boats to be lowered and lie alongside. Colonel Seton of the 74th Highlanders also promptly appeared on deck and took command of the troops. He impressed on the officers the importance of preserving silence and discipline, and gave orders for the men to be paraded on each side of the quarter-deck. The men obeyed as if about to undergo inspection and a party was told off to work the pumps, while another was detailed to help the sailors lower the boats, and yet another to throw the horses overboard.

Captain Wright of the 91st Highlanders, one of the few survivors, wrote:

> Everyone did as he was directed. All received their orders and had them carried out as if the men were embarking instead of going to the bottom; there was only this difference—that I never saw any embarkation conducted with so little noise and confusion.

Unfortunately Captain Salmond, thinking perhaps to get the ship afloat again and to steam nearer the shore, ordered the engines to set the paddles in reverse. The ship then again struck the rocks and tore a large hole in her bottom. Water poured in and put out the fires in her boilers, thus greatly hastening her end. Falling timbers damaged some of the boats, while others stuck in the davits. Only the cutter and two small boats were launched successfully in the ten minutes before the ship broke in two.

Colonel Seton, with drawn sword, stood at the gangway seeing the women and children safely into the cutter. They were ordered to lie off about 150 yards from the rapidly sinking ship. Meanwhile, the soldiers remained quietly drawn up in their ranks, even though, as she broke in two, the main mast and funnel collapsed on the starboard side, crushing many of them. Nor must it be forgotten that these were mostly raw recruits, who had only been in the service a few months.

When the ship broke up, she rapidly began to sink forward, and those who remained on board clustered on the poop at the stern. All, however, remained extremely orderly and quiet. Finally Captain Salmond suggested that everyone who could swim should jump overboard and swim for the boats. Colonel Seton, however, told them that if they did so they would be sure to swamp them and send the women and children to the bottom: he therefore asked them to keep their ranks and they obeyed him. The officers shook hands and said goodbye to each other, immediately after which the ship again broke in two abaft the mainmast. Most of those who had bravely stood to their posts then went down with the ship.

An eyewitness reported:

> Until the vessel disappeared there was not a cry or a murmur from the soldiers or sailors. Those who could swim struck out for the shore, but few ever reached it; most of them either sank from exhaustion, or were devoured by the sharks, or were

dashed to death on the rugged shore near Danger Point, or were entangled in the death-grip of the long arms of seaweed that floated thickly near the coast.

It had all happened very quickly. About twenty minutes after the *Birkenhead* had first struck, all that remained were a few fragments of timber and the mainmast still showing above water. Had Captain Salmond been able to launch the boats before attempting to move the ship and had Colonel Seton set the troops to manufacturing make-shift rafts, it is possible that many more lives might have been saved, but hindsight of this nature, without full knowledge of the facts, is pointless. Of the 631 on board, 438 were drowned. Only 193 were saved, but not a woman or child was lost. For that the 438 died willingly.

Among those who did manage to swim ashore and land at Danger Point was Captain Wright of the 91st Highlanders. With seven men, all of them exhausted after their long swim, he led the way over fifteen miles of barren, rugged coast to the nearest household. There the small party of survivors finally reached safety and succour, and soon the name of the *Birkenhead* reverberated round the world. The Kaiser even ordered an account of the troops' gallant behaviour to be read to all regiments of the German Army as a supreme example of discipline and courage.

With the transition to steam, shipwrecks became less common, but one final hazard remains unmentioned. In 1857 troops were hastily sent to India to quell the Indian Army Mutiny. The *Belleisle* and the *Mauritius* sailed at much the same time. The *Mauritius* had the 93rd, or Sutherland Highlanders on board. When they reached Simon's Town in July the crew mutinied and refused to coal or water the ship. Volunteers from the 93rd, working night and day, succeeded in coaling and watering the ship within five days.

After leaving the Cape the crew continued mutinous in the hope of forcing the Captain to put back to Simon's

Town, but so many of the 93rd at that time were fishermen that they managed to provide eighty-three volunteers able to go aloft in all weathers. These volunteers were given a sailor's pay in addition to their normal pay for the duration of the voyage. As the ship stripped a blade from her propeller she was more often under sail than steam, and was virtually worked to Calcutta by the Sutherland Highlanders unaided. She reached port on the 20th of September just ahead of the *Belleisle*, and the resident Europeans turned out and cheered the 93rd enthusiastically as the transports sailed up river to anchor.

Chapter 9

Medical and Surgical

When one considers the primitive standards of medical and surgical knowledge existing as late as the start of the 20th century, it is only astounding that any wounded ever survived in warfare before then. During the 18th and first half of the 19th century the care of the wounded seems largely to have devolved on the wives and camp followers. Many of these women were quite as skilled and experienced in their treatment of the wounded as the professional army surgeon of the day, whose promotion, as late as 1850, depended as much on his ability to afford the necessary £25 to purchase a set of surgical instruments as on his skill and experience.

Diagnosis was a hit and miss affair, but in obviously severe cases all the surgeons attached to each regiment could do was make the patient as comfortable as possible before his end. Otherwise they could do little more than probe for a musket ball lodged in a non-vital part of the anatomy, then bandage the wound and trust that infection did not ensue. In the case of a severe compound fracture of a limb, amputation was generally their only recourse. The danger of gangrene or infection in such a wound was such that amputation was often the wisest policy. There were, of course, no anaesthetics, no pain killers other than alcohol, no knowledge of germs, hygiene or disinfectants, other than those dictated by common sense.

Fortunately the Scots in the 18th and 19th centuries seem to have been in advance of the rest of the medical profession and to this extent the Highland regiments probably benefited. They certainly benefited by the clean living habits and remarkable physique and endurance of the average Highlander. It was this factor as much as any which must have pulled them through what often seem amazing wounds, even in the light of modern science.

Take for instance the case of Captain Murray of the 42nd, or Black Watch, who was wounded at the capture of Martinique in 1762. A musket ball entered his left side under the lower rib and, as was eventually proved by post-mortem examination, passed through the left lobe of his lung, crossed his chest, and lodged under his right scapula, or shoulder blade. The surgeon who examined him thought him on the point of death and as, was customary in such cases, merely tried to make him comfortable for his last hours. To everyone's astonishment he did not die, and in a few weeks was up and about. Before he reached England his health and appetite were both restored to nearly normal. For the next thirty-two years of his life, however, he was never able to lie down in comfort and always slept in an upright position in bed, supported by pillows. He finally died in 1794, a Lieutenant-General, Colonel of the 72nd regiment and M.P. for Perth.

Even more remarkable was the wound received by Lieutenant Grant of the 42nd at the siege of Charlestown in 1781 and his subsequent recovery. A six-pounder ball struck him on the back at an angle, near the right shoulder, carrying away the entire scapula and several other bones and leaving such a wound that the surgeons merely left him lying on the ground, having made him as comfortable as was possible, for what they assumed must only be a matter of minutes before his death. As he did not die immediately, he was removed to his quarters. The following morning, to the surgeon's amazement, he was not only alive but free of any signs of fever or infection. Thanks to his excellent constitution and healthy way of life, he soon recovered completely and served for many years in good health, dying finally in 1807 as a major in the 78th Highlanders.

An eyewitness account of all that happened to Lieutenant-Colonel Graham of the 42nd, after being wounded when leading a skirmishing party in St. Vincent in the West Indies in 1797, indicates the haphazard treatment of the wounded and also the remarkable stamina and constitution required to survive:

> The first discharge laid Colonel Graham senseless and killed and wounded several of his party: the rest immediately retired. A few men afterwards returned in search of Colonel Graham and . . . believing him dead, rather dragged than carried him over the rough channel of the river till they reached the sea-beach. Observing here that he was still alive, they put him in a blanket, and proceeded in search of a surgeon. After travelling in this manner four miles, I met them and directed the soldiers to carry him to a military post, occupied by a party of the 42nd under my command. All the surgeons were out in the woods with the wounded soldiers and none could be found. Colonel Graham was still insensible. A ball had entered his side and, passing through, had come out under his breast; another, or perhaps the same ball, had shattered two of his fingers. No assistance could be got but that of a soldier's wife, who had been long in the service, and was in the habit of attending sick and wounded soldiers. She washed his wounds and bound them up in such a manner that when a surgeon came and saw the way in which the operation had been performed, he said he could not have done it better and would not unbind the dressings. The Colonel soon afterwards opened his eyes, and though unable to speak for many hours, seemed sensible for what was passing around him . . . He was carried to Kingston, and thence conveyed to England . . . still in a most exhausted state, the wound in his side discharging from both orifices. He went to Edinburgh with little hopes of recovery; but . . . he coughed with great violence and in the exertion threw up a piece of cloth carried in and left by the ball in its passage

through his body. From that day he recovered as by a charm . . . He went to Holland in 1799, when he was severely wounded in the left eye, of which he lost the sight; but a good constitution again triumphed and he accompanied his regiment to Egypt in 1801 . . . In 1822 he was in vigorous health, a Lieutenant-General and Governor of Stirling Castle.

A very similar casualty on St. Vincent was a Lieutenant shot at the top of a steep hill, which he was storming at the head of a small party. A musket ball entered his left breast and passed through his body, coming out at his back. His sergeant, who was greatly attached to him, decided to remove his body for burial, and dragged it by the leg for more than a mile down the hill. At the bottom he left it, deciding to return and bury it that evening. On his return he was extremely startled to hear the supposed corpse speak to him. With the help of a soldier he then carried the Lieutenant back to the camp, where his wound was dressed, and within six weeks he was completely recovered.

There must have been many cases where the wounded were buried under the impression that they were dead. One such instance that was narrowly avoided was recorded by an officer of the 42nd after the landing at Aboukir in 1801:

When the men had laid down to rest after action, I walked to the rear to enquire after some soldiers of my company who had fallen behind, being either killed or wounded. Observing some men digging a hole, and a number of dead bodies lying around, I stept up to one of them, and feeling his temples, felt that they retained some warmth. I then told the soldiers not to bury him, but to carry him to the surgeon, as he did not appear to be quite dead:

'Pho!' said one of them. 'He is as dead as my grandfather who was killed at Culloden.'

And taking the man by the heels he proceeded to drag him to the pit. But I caused him to desist. The wounded man was so horribly disfigured as to justify his companion in the judgement he had formed. A ball had passed through his head, which was in consequence greatly swelled and covered with clotted blood. He was carried to the hospital, where he revived from his swoon, and recovered so rapidly, that in six weeks he was able to do his duty. He lived many years afterwards and was most grateful for my interference.

With so little real knowledge, mistakes in diagnosis were common, even by the surgeons themselves. After the battle with the French outside Alexandria in 1801 it was noted:

Among the Highland wounded were Lieutenant Grant ... who was wounded by a bayonet, which entered one side of his stomach a little below the navel and came out at the other. Lieutenant Stewart ... was wounded in the same part of the body by a musket ball which passed through in a like manner. After the action they lay together in the same tent. Mr. Grant, vomiting and throwing up blood, was considered in immediate danger; Mr. Stewart complained of nothing but a degree of tension and dull pain in the lower abdomen, and the wound was consequently thought to be trifling. The result was quite unexpected. Lieutenant Stewart died at four o'clock the same evening, and Lieutenant Grant was quite well within a fortnight.

Of course, even a Highlander, when hit by a cannon-ball, could not be expected to live long. General Stewart, then a Captain in the 42nd, gives a most graphic account of the death of one of the young soldiers in his company during the fighting in Egypt:

A six pounder shot struck him through both hips as he lay on the ground and made a horrible opening as if he had been cut in two. He cried out:

'God bless you, Captain Stewart, come and give me your hand before I die, and be sure to tell my father and mother that I die like a brave and good soldier, and have saved money for them, which you will send home.'

He said something else, which I could not understand, and dropping his head he expired.

Far more lethal than the musket or cannon-ball were the various fevers which the European, including the Highlander, was liable to contract in the West Indies, Asia, or Africa. Outbreaks of a virulent nature could decimate a regiment, or an army, unless prompt action was taken. Complete and immediate isolation seems to have been the only satisfactory solution, but it is not difficult to imagine the fears of any soldier involved in such an outbreak, aware that if he caught the disease his chances of recovery were small.

After the landing at Aboukir in 1801 plague broke out in the British army camp. A ship from Smyrna, whose crew of thirteen had contracted plague, was run ashore by the two still alive, close to a hospital for sick and wounded. At the sight of the crew the alarm was given, but the disease had already been contracted. It was recorded:

> Every precaution was adopted to prevent any communication with the rest of the army. A line of sentinels was immediately placed round the hospital ground; no intercourse whatever was allowed and if any individual went within the line, they were not permitted to return. Provisions and all necessaries were left on a line of demarcation by those on the outside and then they had removed to some distance, those within came and took them away. By these strict precautions and the unremitting zeal of Dr. Young, who had so ably conducted the hospitals in the West Indies . . . the disease was prevented from spreading . . . Dr. Buchan, Physician to the Forces, had by this time arrived from Edinburgh, where he had been in private practice: and with a fearless and honourable zeal, volunteered to do the duty of the Pest Hospital, though Dr. Finlay and other medical officers had already died of the

plague. To cross this line and enter the den of death, as it was called, and undergo all the consequent privations, exposed, under a canvas tent, to the chilling dews of the night and the fiery heat of an Egyptian mid-day sun, formed no common contrast to the comforts of an Edinburgh practice. Such zeal met with well-merited good fortune and he was very successful in his treatment of the disease. More than half of those who were attacked, that is 400 out of 700 men, recovered under his judicious arrangements. How few recovered under the practice of Turkish surgeons (if surgeons they may be called) is well known. Dr. Buchan further proved his successful practice. He himself recovered from two attacks of the plague; Assistant-Surgeon Webster of the 90th also overcame two attacks.

There was only one case of the plague spreading beyond the confines of the isolation hospital. General Stewart describes this:

A French cavalry deserter had given his cloak to a soldier of the 59th, who was acting as clerk to the Adjutant General's department. The soldier was siezed with the plague the following night and died. Fortunately, from his duty as clerk, he had a small tent exclusively to himself, in which he wrote and slept. This, with all that belonged to him, was burnt to ashes, and thus the pestilence was prevented from spreading to those in the neighbouring tents, who, though quite close, had no personal communication with him. I state the above case more particularly as it is disputed among medical men whether the plague spreads by infection or contact . . . The corporal's tent was twelve yards in the rear of mine, but, fortunately, the nature of the complaint was early discovered and the necessary precautions taken. If it was communicated by air, how could those who lived within a few yards of him, separated only by a piece of canvas, have escaped?

General Stewart described how the attack ended, incidentally providing an illuminating glimpse of the low standards of hygiene prevailing:

At last it became of so mild a nature that, in the month of July, when the cook of the hospital was siezed, it was so little a fever that he never gave up his work, nor complained, until he found it necessary to apply for some dressings when the sores occasioned by the disease had suppurated. The plague is always more violent in cold weather, but as the hot season approaches, it abates, and when the temperature has reached the maximum, it disappears altogether. On the other hand, the yellow fever of New York, generated by heat, is destroyed by cold. As to the fever of the West Indies, it appears and disappears without an visible cause.

Although generally healthier than most troops in the British army and with extremely hardy constitutions, quite apart from the benefits of the kilt, already outlined, the Highlanders were no more immune to plague, or fevers. They could also be badly affected by an abrupt change of diet. When the second battalion of the 78th, or Ross-shire Buffs was raised in 1804 they were at first stationed in Kent. Many of the finest looking of the 600 young Highlanders were attacked by boils and inflammations attributable directly to the transition from a diet of barley, oatmeal and vegetables to meat. Some of them were unable to hold their food down and it was not until the following year that they became acclimatized to the new diet.

Boils and inflammations, however painful, are not normally lethal. The plague, the yellow fever of New York and the West Indies fever were all killers, but the latter was the worst of the lot, as shown by the figures concerning the 92nd, or Gordon Highlanders, who arrived in Jamaica on June 2nd, 1819. They were the first Highland regiment to be stationed there and they were at once attacked by this fever in its most virulent form. The sickness was so bad and so general that, in August, orders were given to disperse the Regiment, but even so the course of the infection was not halted. Between the 24th of June and the 24th of December the Regiment lost 10 officers,

13 sergeants, 8 drummers and 254 rank and file. This considerably exceeded the entire number killed in all the Regiment's many engagements from its formation in 1794 through to Waterloo in 1815.

During the first half of the 19th century medical knowledge began to advance slowly, but a great deal remained guesswork. Anyone wounded internally was generally considered beyond hope, but they did not necessarily always die. Among the officers wounded at the battle of Toulouse in 1814, for instance, was Captain Donald MacQueen of the 74th, who had already been wounded nine times in nine engagements. This time he was shot through both lungs. His foster-brother, Private John Gillanders, of the 74th, who had joined with him when he received his commission, picked him up and carried him off the battlefield and tried vainly to find room for him in a nearby hut, which was packed with wounded officers. Eventually Brigadier Thomas Brisbane, though badly wounded himself, was moved by Private Gillanders' entreaties and gave up his bed. It says much for Gillanders' care and his own constitution that MacQueen recovered and lived until 1830, ending his days as a Major and Military Knight of Windsor.

It was not until Sir James Simpson introduced the use of chloroform as an anaesthetic in 1847 that the way was opened to real progress in medical knowledge and surgical skill. This enabled surgeons for the first time to operate painlessly and without the haste which had previously been necessary. It also meant that abdominal operations and major surgery, which had previously been impossible, could now be undertaken for the first time.

Writing of his experiences with the 93rd Highlanders, Surgeon General William Munro mentioned an incident in South Africa in about 1846, before the introduction of chloroform, which illustrates how much guesswork was involved at that time. He recorded:

> Colour Sergeant Donald Mackay and a private of the 91st Highlanders left camp without leave, taking one of the sergeant's horses with them to bring in green forage . . . Three Kaffirs, who had been lying concealed in the tall oats, one armed with a gun and the others with assegais, sprang upon them. The one with the gun was nearest Mackay, who, perceiving that his only chance was to close with his enemy, rushed forward with that object, but, just as he extended his hand to grasp the barrel of the gun, the Kaffir fired, the muzzle of the weapon almost touching the sergeant's body as he did so. Though Mackay felt he was wounded, he grappled with the Kaffir and after a short struggle wrested the gun out of his hands and clubbing it struck him a blow on the head which killed him . . .

The private who had accompanied him was killed by the other two Kaffirs, but the sergeant was able to mount his horse and make good his escape. Surgeon General Munro continued:

> I was standing at the door of my hut and saw Mackay gallop in and dismount. To my surprise he walked straight up to me and saluting with one hand, while he pressed the other to his side, said, very quietly:
>
> 'I am badly wounded, sir.'
>
> He then turned and walked steadily to the hospital, but fainted as we laid him down on a cot. On removing his clothes I found that he had been shot right through the abdomen. The bullet had entered a little to the left of the umbilicus and passed straight through and made its exit just below the rim of the ilium, or pelvis, making a clean circular hole in the bone into which my finger exactly fitted. The skin round the wound was much scorched showing that the muzzle of the gun must have been close to the point of entry. I quite expected that death would follow such a wound in a few hours, for it seemed to me impossible that a bullet could pass through the abdomen without injuring the bowels, but such was the case and when the scorched skin dropped off, I could distinctly see the bowels

lying uninjured and in their usual position. Within two months Mackay was quite recovered and able to resume his duty and was discharged before the battalion left the frontier in 1847. In 1883 he was still alive and well at the age of 76.

Writing later, on the subject of the Crimean forces, Surgeon General Munro admitted:

> No army ever took the field, or landed in a hostile country with the prospect—nay certainty—of immediate battle, so unprepared and so imperfectly supplied with medical and surgical equipment as did our small, but splendid Crimean army. The men that filled its ranks were the finest soldiers that I ever saw in stature, physique and appearance . . . We had a large number of regimental medical officers, but no regimental hospitals, and there were no field hospitals with proper staff of attendants. We had no ambulance for sick or wounded.
>
> The regimental hospital was represented by one bell tent and the medical and surgical equipment by a pair of panniers containing a small case of surgical instruments, a few medicines, a small supply of dressings, a tin or two of beef tea, some arrowroot and sugar and a quart of brandy, also the medical and surgical records of the regiment, and these panniers were carried by a wretched pony miserably out of condition. Most of the instruments were the private property of the surgeon paid for out of his own pocket, £25, as one of the conditions attached to promotion. The only means of carrying sick and wounded men, ten hand stretchers entrusted to the band. One sergeant, three orderlies, and a horse-keeper were provided by the regiment. In the event of battle the transports were at hand, but these were not prepared for the reception of the wounded and we had no such thing as a hospital ship.

Even by 1854 the army had a long way to go before it began to be organized to deal with the sick. The example set by Florence Nightingale paved the way for future improvements, but not before time. Just prior to the battle of Alma the Principal Medical Officer of the army had issued a circular practically prohibiting the use of chloroform, in spite of which Surgeon Munro, as he then was, used it for every operation he performed. The 93rd Highlanders were indeed fortunate in their surgeon. Yet if they recovered it was not primarily to him they owed it, but to their own clean living and strong constitutions. The hardiness of the Highlander generally seems to have triumphed, even over disease or wounds.

Chapter 10

Second Sight

In primitive communities untouched by civilization a firm belief in ghosts is still common. Some individuals may also possess a remarkable gift for thought transference, occasionally combined with an ability to foretell the future. The Highlanders termed this ability second sight and accepted it as something not particularly unusual, but also as something it was not wise to scoff at unduly. With the modern need to rationalize and investigate everything this is now termed Extra Sensory Perception, or E.S.P. for short, and is the subject of serious study by various bodies around the world.

There are two apparently well-authenticated accounts of second sight, or presentiments of approaching death, connected with the battle of Ticonderoga in North America in 1758, when the 42nd Royal Highland Regiment, or Black Watch, attacked the well fortified stronghold of St. Louis, also known by its Indian name of Ticonderoga. The attack itself was pressed home with great bravery on the part of the Black Watch. Their casualties were 8 officers, 9 sergeants, and 297 men killed, and 17 officers, 10 sergeants and 306 men wounded, or a total of 647.

Describing the battle afterwards Lieutenant William Grant wrote:

> The attack began a little past one in the afternoon, and about two, the fire became general on both sides, which was exceedingly heavy and without any intermission, insomuch

that the oldest soldier present never saw so furious and incessant a fire. The affair at Fontenoy was nothing to it; I saw both. We laboured under insurmountable difficulties. The enemy's breastwork was about nine or ten feet high, upon the top of which they had plenty of wall-pieces fixed, and which was well lined inside with small-arms. But the difficult access to their lines was what gave them a fatal advantage over us. They took care to cut down monstrous large oak trees, which covered all the ground from the foot of their breastwork about the distance of a cannon shot every way in their front. This not only broke our ranks, and made it impossible for us to keep order but put it entirely out of our power to advance till we cut our way through. I have seen men behave with courage and resolution before now, but such determined bravery can hardly have been equalled in any part of the history of ancient Rome. Even those who were mortally wounded cried aloud to their companions not to mind, or lose a thought upon them, but to follow their officers, and to mind the honour of their country. Nay, their ardour was such, that it was difficult to bring them off. They paid dearly for their intrepidity. The remains of the regiment had the honour to cover the retreat of the army and brought off the wounded, as we did at Fontenoy. When shall we have so fine a regiment again? I hope we shall be allowed to recruit.

An English officer of the 55th, or Lord Howe's regiment, who witnessed the attack wrote:

With a mixture of esteem, grief and envy, I consider the great loss and immortal glory acquired by the Scots Highlanders in the late bloody affair. Impatient for orders, they rushed forward to the entrenchments, which many of them actually mounted. They appeared like lions breaking their chains. Their intrepidity was rather animated than damped by seeing their comrades fall on every side. I have only to say that they seemed more anxious to revenge the cause of their deceased friends, than careful to avoid the same fate. By their assistance we expect soon to give a good account of the enemy and ourselves. There is much harmony and friendship between us.

General Stewart of Garth recorded one case of presentiment of approaching death prior to Ticonderoga. He noted:

> One of the Lieutenants killed that day was remarked for great firmness of character and good sense. Yet he could not shake off a presentiment that siezed him the morning of the action that he would be killed. He gave some directions about his family affairs to Captain Stewart of Urrard and Lieutenant Farquharson. Captain Stewart endeavoured to remove this impression; but when he found that his arguments had no effect, he recommended him to exchange his turn of duty, to which he answered:
>
> 'I know you are my friend, otherwise I would consider your proposal an insult.'
>
> He marched at the head of the grenadier company and was shot through the breast by the first discharge.

The famous story connected with Ticonderoga, however, concerns Major Duncan Campbell of Inverawe. It has been the subject of learned addresses to the Historical Association of New York and of pamphlets, articles and stories, as well as being perpetuated in verse by Robert Louis Stevenson. Inevitably legends have grown up around it obscuring the truth, or at the least distorting it over the years, yet it appears to be an authentic instance of second sight, E.S.P., or call it what you will.

The true story, or as near as one can get to it, seems to have begun on a summer evening in 1755, when Major Duncan Campbell was out on the slopes of Ben Cruachan above his ancient fortified home of Inverawe. A badly frightened man in the last stages of exhaustion staggered up to him and begged for shelter. He explained that he had accidentally slain a man in an affray and was now being pursued by friends of the dead man, intent on killing him in revenge.

In a moment of pity Campbell of Inverawe promised to shelter him.

'Swear on your dirk!' cried the stranger.

'I swear by the word of an Inverawe, which never failed friend or foe yet,' replied Campbell proudly.

He then led the exhausted man to a cave in the hillside known only to his family. The entrance was as small as a fox's earth, but inside were fair-sized rooms, which included a spring of fresh water. Tradition held that Wallace and Bruce had both sheltered there.

On Inverawe's return home he found armed men awaiting him. He was horrified to learn that the man he was protecting had killed his dearly loved foster-brother, Donald, but, remembering his oath, he did not betray the fugitive to those searching for him. Deeply disturbed, he retired to try to sleep, when suddenly the ghost of his foster-brother appeared before him, pale and blood-spattered, stern of aspect, with his fair hair clotted with gore.

'Inverawe, shield not the murderer. Blood must flow for blood,' the apparition intoned sternly, before disappearing.

After a sleepless night, Inverawe visited the cave next morning and told the man he must make his escape as best he could for he could shelter him no longer. The other reminded him of his oath and, much against his will, Inverawe felt obliged to stand by his word and allow him to stay.

That night the ghost of his foster-brother appeared again and once more spoke the fateful words:

'Inverawe, shield not the murderer. Blood must flow for blood.'

This was altogether too much for Inverawe and after another sleepless night he went to the cave to tell the fugitive that he must leave, only to find that he had already fled under cover of darkness. Much relieved, he returned home, but his relief proved premature. That night the apparition appeared again, still ghastly pale, but seeming less stern than before. In sorrowful tones came the warning:

'Farwell, Inverawe. Farewell, till we meet at Ticonderoga.'

The strange name remained fixed in Campbell of Inverawe's mind, and for many months, as may be imagined, he was a very worried man. However, he had much to occupy him. As Major in the Black Watch, in which his son John was a Captain, he was soon busy preparing for the Regiment to sail for North America, where war had broken out between the English and French. In 1756 the Black Watch embarked from Greenock and in June landed at New York. From there they moved to Albany where they were quartered for most of 1757.

One night in Albany in the mess Major Campbell revealed the entire story to the officers assembled round the table after dinner. It is easy to imagine the impression it made as the port circulated and the snuff was passed round. When he had finished he made them promise to let him know at once if they heard the name. Hence there was general consternation when it was learned that the Indian name of Fort St. Louis, which they were sent to attack in July 1758, was Ticonderoga. Lieutenant-Colonel Francis Grant, the commanding officer persuaded the other officers to keep the news from him, and they referred to it by its French name. On the morning of the attack, however, he appeared with haggard gaze, declaring:

'You have deceived me. I have seen him. He came to my tent last night. This is Ticonderoga. I shall die today.'

So much for the story. In fact he does not seem to have been killed instantly, as one feels he should have been. He was wounded in the arm. With the aid of modern drugs or surgery there is little doubt that he would have been saved. As it was, infection set in and after a few days he died. He was buried nearby and his grave is still visible. Just how much of the story, or the legends that have grown around this event, it is reasonable to believe is hard to decide. This is by no means the end of it.

On the day of the attack on Fort Ticonderoga in North America, two ladies, Miss Campbell of Ederein and her sister were walking from Kilmalieu to Inveraray and had reached the then new bridge over the Aray. One of them happened to look up at the sky. She called to her sister to look also. Both saw what looked like a siege in progress. They saw the different regiments with their colours and recognized their friends amongst the Highlanders. They saw Inverawe and his son fall, as well as others whom they knew. When they reached Inveraray they told their friends of the vision they had just seen. They also took down the names of those they had seen fall and the time and date of the occurrence.

They were not uncorroborated. The well-known Danish physician, Sir William Hart, together with an Englishman and a servant, walking round the Castle of Inveraray saw the same phenomenon and confirmed the statements made by the two ladies. Weeks later the Gazette also confirmed them with its account of the attack at Ticonderoga and every detail of their vision was found to be correct. Just where a contemporary note of this story may be found, however, is another matter. When every detail is taken into account in all these stories about Ticonderoga, however, it would still appear that at least one person had a genuine presentiment of his approaching death that day.

An interesting account of an apparently genuine case of second sight was recorded in the year 1775, when Lord Breadalbane was visited by one of his tenants. The man was upset at the loss of his son, whom he said had been killed in battle, even mentioning the day on which it had happened. Lord Breadalbane assured him that this was quite impossible, as not only had there been no news of any battle, but there was not even any news of any war in progress. The tenant refused to be reassured, maintaining that he had seen his son lying dead and many officers and soldiers dead around him. Finally Lord Breadalbane gave up trying to convince him that he was imagining it all and left him. Some weeks later, when the account of the Battle of Bunker's

Hill was announced he was astonished to learn that the son had indeed been killed at the time and in the manner in which the father had described to him.

After all this it comes almost as something of a relief to read General Stewart's account of the private in the 2nd battalion of the 73rd, or Macleod's Highlanders, who was with them in 1780 when they were defending Gibraltar against the Spanish:

> (He) was threatened with punishment, as a false prophet, having declared that he had the second sight (although it proved a false one) by which he foresaw the surrender of the fortress. However, the commander was too much of an enlightened soldier to fear or punish such absurd predictions and after a short confinement the poor fellow was released with a caution not to utter any more of his dreams until the event he had foreseen should have been determined by the occurrence.

General Stewart did, however, record another instance of a presentiment of death in battle:

> Lieutenant-Colonel Malcolm, son of Sir James Malcolm of Lochore in the county of Kinross, was appointed in the year 1794 to command a small corps of coloured and black troops, who had entered our service in Guadeloupe and Martinique. On every occasion they conducted themselves with great spirit and proved how much discipline judiciously administered can accomplish even with such materials; for, while Colonel Malcolm commanded, he so secured their attachment to his person, that when he fell, they crowded round him, loudly lamenting their loss, which had indeed greater effect upon them than was at first apprehended, for their spirit seemed to die without their leader, and they never afterwards distinguished themselves. This officer, with all his intrepidity and spirit, could not conquer a presentiment which siezed him on the night of the attack, that he was then to fall. While marching forward he frequently mentioned to General Hope his firm

belief in his fate, which no argument could shake. The moment he reached the battery, he was struck by a grape-shot.

A feature of these cases of presentiment almost always seems to have been the lack of any fear, indeed rather the opposite. Surgeon General Munro gives two instances from the 93rd, or Sutherland Highlanders in the Indian Mutiny in 1857:

When Sir Colin Campbell rode up to the regiment and desired the men to fall in to assault the Sha Najaf, one of the men (Private McLeod) was slow in taking his place in the ranks. His comrades in impatience called to him:

'Come along, man, you're surely no feared.'

The imputation he indignantly denied, saying:

'No, I'm no feared an' I'll show ye that there's nae white feather aboot me, but I ken weel I'm goin' to my death.'

Not many minutes afterwards when close to the wall of the Sha Najaf, a ball passed through his head and he fell dead.

The other instance Surgeon General Munro gives reads:

As the 93rd was falling in for the assault on the Begum Koti at Lucknow, a young private, David Ross, took off his Crimean medal and handed it to his brother, who was a sergeant in the regiment, saying as he did so:

'Here, John, send this home to our mother—I shall be killed today.'

He *was* killed, while fighting bravely, and scarcely half an hour after he had handed his medal to his brother.

One last case in 1880 recorded in the history of 92nd, or Gordon Highlanders has features of interest. Sergeant MacFadyean related how, on August 23rd, during the march to Kandahar, Private Allan MacDonald of G Company, a native of the Island of Coll, in Argyllshire, told him in confidence of a dream which had deeply impressed him.

He said he had dreamed the previous night that he was in battle when a bullet struck him in the forehead and that as it was being extracted he died. The sergeant did his best to cheer him up without success. He had forgotten the whole affair when, on August 28th, Private MacDonald told him that the dream had been repeated. Shortly before capturing the enemy's guns at the battle of Kandahar that day, the sergeant seeing him alive called out:

'Hullo, Allan, you are still safe, I see.'

'Oh, yes,' he answered with a smile. 'I'm all right, yet.'

Despite this his dream was fulfilled in every detail. One of the last shots from the hill struck Private MacDonald in the forehead and a day or two later, as the bullet was being extracted, he died under the surgeon's hands.

Chapter 11

Wives and Camp Followers

It is an old saying with a great deal of truth in it that the female of the species is more deadly than the male. Taking into account the fact that the Highlanders made quite outstanding soldiers, the corollary is plain. The Highlanders' wives and camp followers were generally of quite remarkable calibre. The Rev. Mr. John Grant, Minister of Tomintoul, outlined very lucidly the career of a camp follower, soldier's wife and widow, whom he knew well in 1790, as follows:

> In personal respect and fortune at the head of the inhabitants (of Tomintoul) must be ranked Mrs. M'Kenzie, of the best inn at the sign of the horns. This heroine began her career of celebrity in the accommodating disposition of an easy virtue, at the age of 14 in the year 1745. That year saw her in Flanders, caressing and caressed. Superior to the little prejudices of her sex she relinquished the first object of her affection and attached herself to a personage high in the military department. After a campaign or two spent in acquiring a knowledge of man and the world, Scotland saw her again; but wearied of the inactivity of rural retirement she then married and made her husband enlist in the Royal Highlanders at the commencement of the war in 1756. With him she navigated the Atlantic and sallied forth on American ground in quest of adventures, equally prepared to meet her friends, or encounter her enemies in the fields of Venus or Mars as occasion offered. At the conclusion of the war she revisited her native country. After a variety of vicissitudes in Germany, France, Holland, England, Ireland, Scotland, America and the West Indies her

anchor is now moored on dry land in the village of Tamnetoul. It might be imagined that such extremes of climate, so many rugged paths, so many severe bruises, as she must have experienced in her progress through life would have impaired her health, especially when it is considered that she added 24 children to the aggregate of general births, beside some homunculi that stopped short in their passage. Wonderful, however, as it may appear, at this moment she is as fit for her usual active life as ever; and except 2 or 3 grey hairs vegetating from a mole upon one of her cheeks, that formerly set off a high ruddy complexion, she still retains all the apparent freshness and vigour of youth.

The skill in nursing of many of the wives and camp followers has already been mentioned. Particular reference was made to a soldier's wife who bandaged the wound Colonel Graham received in 1797 with the 42nd at St. Vincent, when the surgeon admitted that he could not have done better. General Stewart referred to her as a woman of uncommon character and continued: 'She had been long a follower of the camp and had acquired some of its manners. While she was so good and useful a nurse in quarters she was also bold and fearless in the field.'

He instanced an occasion when an attack was to be made:

> I directed that her husband, who was in my company, should remain behind to take charge of the men's knapsacks, which they had thrown off to be light for the advance up the hill, as I did not wish to have him exposed to danger on account of his wife and family. He obeyed his orders and remained with his charge, but his wife, believing herself not to be included in those injunctions pushed forward to the assault. When the enemy had been beaten from the third redoubt, I was standing giving some directions to the men and preparing to push on to the fourth and last redoubt, when I found myself tapped in the shoulder and turning round saw my Amazonian friend standing with her clothes tucked up to her knees; and siezing my hand she exclaimed:

'Well done my Highland lads! See how the brigands scamper like so many deer!'

'Come,' she added. 'Let us drive them from yonder hill.'

On inquiry I found that she had been in the hottest fire cheering and animating the men and when the action was over she was as active as any of the surgeons in assisting the wounded.

In his history of the Gordon Highlanders Colonel Greenhill Gardyne describes the life of a military wife:

During their marches the troops were accompanied by the wives and children of the N.C. officers and soldiers, who received rations; and though they sometimes caused anxiety, both to their husbands and the commanding officer, were of great use in nursing the sick, washing the linen of the officers and men, etc., while their presence gave something of a home-like appearance to the camp or cantonments. They generally had donkeys, which they rode, or which carried panniers with their children and possessions; they were capital foragers, were as full of *esprit-de-corps* as the men, and bore the fatigues of a campaign with the patient fortitude of their sex. I knew well an old lady who used to tell with pride how, when a sudden order to march came, while the linen of the men she washed for was in the tub, she took advantage of the fact that she was billetted on a wood merchant to make a roaring fire, and succeeded in giving every man his dry shirt as he stood on parade, emerging like Wellington at Fuentes d'Onor, undefeated by the difficulties of the situation. She gave brandy to the wounded in the ensuing engagement, made her husband's breakfast before the fight of the next day, and ended her eventful life as the respected hostess of a hotel in Argyllshire.

When the Gordon Highlanders were stationed at Weeley Barracks, Colchester in 1804, the married men were allowed to live in Government huts outside barracks, but their wives sometimes abused this privilege by selling liquor and allowing disorderly conduct. Two extracts from the Regimental Orders demonstrate this point:

Major Cameron was perfectly shocked at the infamous scene of gambling he witnessed today in the rear of the centre huts of the 92nd Regiment.

On account of the irregularities allowed by Private M'Kean, his hut is to be burned down by the pioneers, and if Mrs. M'Kean continues these disgraceful scenes, she will be drummed out of the regiment.

In 1807, when the 92nd were in Denmark, they found that the Scots and Danes had a good deal in common, particularly a liking for music and liquor. There was a notable increase in drunkenness, which Colonel Napier attributed to women bringing brandy and wine in from the neighbouring town of Roskeld. Two further extracts from Regimental Orders at the time indicate the Colonel's methods of dealing with the situation: 'Mrs. Semple of the 1st Company, having been found in the act, her provisions are stopped.' In the case of another wife, whose conduct was even more heinous: 'It was the intention of Lt.-Colonel Napier that she should be drummed through the quarters of the regiment, but out of respect for the character of her husband, the Lieutenant-Colonel will be satisfied with her disappearance for ever—and he gives her forty-eight hours to do so.'

The wives had to share all the sufferings and hardships of their husbands and sometimes these proved too much for them. During the retreat to Corunna in 1808, for instance, there were hardships in plenty. The troops were living on raw turnips, barefoot in the bitter cold. According to the history of the 92nd: 'On this march the wife of Sergeant Charles MacGregor with her three boys, who were carried in creels on a donkey, fell out of the line and were never more heard of.'

Considering how much trouble they could cause at times, quite apart from the natural anxiety of the men concerning them, it is understandable that commanding officers were often prejudiced against marriage. Part of a 92nd Regimental Order for June 9th, 1810, reads: 'From the strong certificate the commanding officer has had of the young woman and from Private John Campbell's own good character, he has granted permission to marry; at the same time it is forming a connection which he strongly wishes to recommend every soldier to avoid, and his consent can never be obtained, but when the most unquestionable certificate can be produced of the moral good character of the female.'

The number of wives per company was limited and tended to vary from regiment to regiment according to circumstances, but was seldom more than six. One very good reason for restricting the number of soldiers' wives, especially on a campaign, was simply the difficulty of accommodation. This applied equally to the wives of N.C.O.s. Sergeant Anton, of the 42nd, or Black Watch, made this plain in his account of what happened when he and his wife first joined the Regiment in the Peninsula. After reporting for duty, he recorded:

> I set about looking for some accommodation for my wife, for we had not yet been accustomed to lie in the open field, as in bivouac, nor even seen the like, and the tent was far from comfortable for a poor wearied young woman. The names of seventeen men were on the roll of the tent besides myself, so that it may easily be guessed how crowded it must have been had the whole been off duty, but this was seldom the case. However, as no other shelter was to be had we took a berth under it. Eleven soldiers lay in it that night, along with us, all stretched with their feet to the centre and their heads to the curtain of the tent. Every man's knapsack below his head and his clothes and accoutrements on his body; the one half of the blankets under, and the other spread over the whole, so that we all lay in one bed. Often did my poor wife look up at the thin canvas that screened her face from the night dew and wish for the approaching morn. It was announced, at last, before daybreak, by an exclamation of 'Rouse!' . . . I now set about erecting a hut for

myself and wife, resolving, if possible, not to mix blankets with so many bed-fellows again. This I was the more anxious to do, because at that time the whole of the men were affected with an eruption on their skin similar to the itch and their clothing was in a filthy state, owing to its seldom being shifted and always kept on during the night.

The sergeant described the building of the hut, the first of several similar edifices he constructed for his wife and himself, as follows:

With the help of a few willing hands, I finished the hut in the course of the day, so that it served for a temporary shelter, and prevented myself and my wife depriving the men of their very limited accommodation in the tent. When I stretched myself down at night in my new habitation, my head rested against one end, while my feet touched the other, at which was the entrance; my wife's apron being hung as a substitute for a door; a couple of pins on each side served for lock and hinges; and feeble as that barrier was, none of the men entered when that was suspended, and we might have left it to its own keeping from morning to night without an article being abstracted; thieving was indeed unknown in the Regiment.

On one occasion a sudden fierce gale blew down one of their huts in the night and in the morning they discovered:

Our day's provisions were among the articles missing, and this was far from being a comfortable look out for the day, as I had to mount the advanced picquet that morning; however we had a little money, and, scarce as bread was, it was to be had for a good price.

The advanced picquet was more than two miles from the camp, and as I had not taken any provision with me for the day, my wife bought a small loaf and a little wine; this last she mulled and mixed with some of the bread, and was bringing to me; but in her too great anxiety to reach me soon, by short roads, she slipped on one of the steep banks, and rolled down a considerable declivity. Fortunately she was not hurt, but heartily vexed at her own mishap, returned to the camp, made a fresh purchase and again hastened to me . . . she returned to camp gratified at having provided me with an unexpected and comfortable refreshment.

When a regiment was in action the wife was often close behind, as has been noted. After the battle of Nivelle on November 10th, 1813, Sergeant Anton recorded:

> We bivouacked in the field until morning, and fortunately for us the night was fair, although cold and frosty. This was the first night on which my wife and I had to lie down with no other covering than a blanket between us and the sky, but we had many worse nights than this afterwards and worse fields before us.

Harrowing scenes sometimes took place on the battlefield when the battle was over, as wives searched anxiously for their husbands among the wounded and dead. When a soldier was killed his widow was usually forced to marry another protector, or lose her virtue altogether, for generally on his death her rations ceased and there was no other way for her to survive. An example of this sort of scene was recorded after the battle of Toulouse among the ranks of the 42nd, or Black Watch:

> Here fell Cunninghame, a corporal in the grenadier company, a man much esteemed in the regiment; he was a married man, but young, and was interred before his wife entered the dear-bought field; but she had heard his fate and flew, in spite of every opposition to the field; she looked around the yet unburied soldiers to find her own, but she found him not. She flew to the place where the wreck of the regiment lay in the field.
>
> 'Tell me,' she asked, 'Where Cunninghame is laid that I may see him and lay him in the grave with my own hand.'

> A tear rose in the soldier's eye as he pointed towards the place and twenty men started up to accompany her to the spot, for they respected the man and esteemed the woman. They lifted the corpse; the wounds were in his breast; she washed them, and pressing his cold lips to hers, wept over him, wrapped the body in a blanket, and the soldiers consigned it to the grave . . . The officer who commanded the company to which Cunninghame belonged having been severely wounded, sent for the widow; she became his sick nurse and under his protection was restored in decent respectability to her home.

From the wife's viewpoint it must often have been extremely hard to know where her duty to her husband lay. Sergeant Anton gives an account of his wife's dilemma on the day peace was declared in April 1814, when the regiment moved on without him and she had to decide either to move on with them, or stay and wait for him:

> On the 15th the accounts of peace were made known to the army and were received with every demonstration of joy . . . and as no movement was expected that day, I obtained leave to return to Toulouse in order to purchase some articles for the company to which I was attached.
>
> Having settled my affairs as speedily as possible at Toulouse I made all haste to return to the regiment, but to my astonishment on approaching the place which I had left echoing with the busy hum of a hundred voices, I found all hushed in solitary silence. I proceeded up the avenue, where the embers of the expiring fires smoked against the walls; not a soldier was to be seen . . . at last as I approached the door (of the farmhouse) I saw my wife in tears, sitting on my knapsack. My approach dispelled her grief, her heart leaped with joy and springing up, she embraced me.
>
> We now had to find out the place to which the regiment had proceeded; and after pursuing the supposed route till after sunset, without any information whether right or wrong, we came to a small village occupied by the 74th regiment and from the men of their corps met with a very friendly reception and

were made welcome to quarters during the night. Early next morning as we were about to proceed in search of our own regiment, the sound of the bagpipe struck our ears and in a few minutes its welcome notes directed us to the regiment.

The army was often remarkably insensitive about the sufferings of wives. For example, when the 42nd embarked from Ireland for Ostend in May 1815, just prior to Waterloo, four wives were permitted to follow each company and they were provided with accommodation on board ship to Ostend. Thereafter it was recorded:

> Boats lay on the canal, ready to convey us into the interior of the country; but as we were stepping on board, an order was received, that only two women would be allowed to proceed with each company. This was a great disappointment, and no small cause of grief to those who had to return without any preparation for such an unexpected separation, or any provision, but that which the liberality of their country might allow, or the hand of charity present to carry them to their distant home. Those who had gotten on board of the boats waiting for our conveyance were turned out, notwithstanding their sighs and tears, given in charge to a guard, and quartered in a barrack at Ostend. Meanwhile we moved slowly up the canal and left the poor weeping women behind to form their future plans . . . and make arrangements for following the fortunes of their husbands . . .
>
> We had only been two days in Ghent, when the women left at Ostend found their way to the regiment; they were again conveyed back to the same place from which they escaped, and there closely watched; Yet in a week or two they eluded the vigilance of the sentries and joined their husbands once more, and as no official reports were made to their prejudice, they followed the fortunes of their husbands during the campaign along with those who boasted the privilege.

If the army could be insensitive to the sufferings of the Highland soldiers' wives, it was nothing to the treatment sometimes meted out to their widows by the civil authorities. Describing the Strathnaver Clearance of 1819, the Reverend Mr. Donald Sage recorded in his diary:

> At an early hour . . . Mr. Sellar (The Duke of Sutherland's factor) . . . commenced work . . . Their plan of operations was to clear the cottages of inmates, giving them about half an hour to pack up and carry their furniture off and then set the cottages on fire. To this plan they ruthlessly adhered, without the slightest regard to any obstacle that might arise in carrying out its execution . . . At Grumbeg lived a soldier's widow, Henny Munro . . . She was a joyous, cheery old creature; so inoffensive, moreover and so contented and brimful of goodwill that all who got acquainted with old Henny Munro could only desire to do her a good turn, were it merely for the warm and hearty expressions of gratitude with which it was received . . .
>
> Mr. Sellar and his iron-hearted attendants approached the residence of the soldier's widow. Henny stood up to plead for her furniture—the coarsest and most valueless that well could be, but still her earthly all . . . She was told with an oath that if she did not take her trumpery off within half an hour it would be burned. The poor widow had only to task the remains of her bodily strength and address herself to the work of dragging her chests, beds, presses and stools out of the door and placing them at the gable of her cottage. No sooner was her task accomplished than the torch was applied, the widow's hut, built of very combustible material speedily ignited . . . The wind unfortunately blew in the direction of the furniture and the flame, lighting upon it, speedily reduced it to ashes . . .

Another even feebler widow evicted on this occasion died two days later and the following year Mr. Sellar was tried for murder in Inverness, but the trial proved to be a travesty of justice, held in English although all the witnesses spoke Gaelic, and it was a foregone conclusion that he would be acquitted, as indeed he was. Evictions of the wives, widows, parents and families of serving Highland soldiers, as well as of pensioners, continued apace with inevitably disastrous effects on recruiting.

In spite of this the standard of the wives accompanying the Highland regiments does not seem to have changed greatly by the time of the Crimean War, in 1854. Surgeon General William Munro particularly noted the conduct of one woman when the 93rd were in action and the Turkish regiment on their flank fled at the approach of the enemy:

> When the Turks turned tail and ran down the hill a camp follower of the regiment, a stalwart Scotch wife, was employed at the time washing some articles of clothing beside a little stream that flowed through a vineyard at the base of the hill on the crest of which the 93rd stood in line, apparently and really, I believe, quite unconcerned about the battle and unmoved by the sound of round shot which passed over her head. When she saw the Turks rushing down the hill and amongst the tents she thought they were bent on plunder, and watched them for a minutes with suspicious eye; but when they swept past her, and trampled on the things which, being washed, she had spread out to dry, she broke into a towering rage, and siezing a large stick that lay on the ground near her, laid about her right and left in protection of her property. When she understood that the Turks were bolting from the battle and had deserted her own regiment which she saw standing firm upon the hill above, she laughed in scorn, and again applied her stick, striking heavily, at the same time using her tongue, a sharp weapon at times, she abused the flying 'Johnnies' roundly in braid Scotch to the great amusement of the men of her own regiment, who encouraged by applauding her.
>
> She was a stalwart wife, large and massive, with brawny arms and hands as hard as horn. Her face, though bronzed and weather-beaten and deeply freckled, was comely, and lighted up by a pair of kindly hazel eyes. Her voice was soft and low when she 'wasna angered,' and within her capacious bosom beat a tender, honest heart. I knew her well and knew she was always ready to do a kindness to anyone in need. She remained

in the Crimea during the first part of the winter, till the bad weather came on, and was then sent to Scutari, from whence, at the conclusion of the war, she returned to England, and taking her old husband, who was discharged and pensioned, under her care again (for she was the better man of the two) settled somewhere in the old countrie. After her exploits at Balaklava she was invariably spoken of as Kokana Smith, the equivalent of Lady, and treated with great respect by the Turks.

Of course the camp followers with whom the Highlanders had to deal were not always on their own side. During the Second Kaffir War in 1850 the remarkable number of Hottentot women around the column and their behaviour began to arouse suspicion in the 91st. The Colonel made inquiries about their movements and failing to receive satisfactory answers ordered them to be searched by the Fingoes, or native auxiliaries:

> To the indignation of all, quantities of ammunition were found secreted in their bundles, or on their persons, for the undoubted purpose of being clandestinely conveyed to the rebels. On one woman ninety-five rounds of government ammunition were found; on another eighty; others had smaller quantities and one carried a canister of loose powder and a bullet mould and turnscrew . . . It was with the greatest difficulty that the women were rescued from the infuriated Fingoes, who would have assegaied them on the spot, but for the interference of the officers: they were sent back prisoners to Beaufort . . . Ammunition and food it was accidentally found had been regularly forwarded to them by the Tottie women in our own camps—fed by the way at Government expense who under the pretence of collecting firewood in the bush hid their supplies in certain assigned spots from which they were secretly taken away at night by the rebels.

Nor were the enemy camp followers always to be found in such passive roles. During the fighting after the Indian Mutiny in 1857 the 42nd, or Black Watch, encountered an unusual case. When the battle of Secunderabagh had nearly been successfully concluded a regimental historian recorded:

> Many of the soldiers lay down under a large peepul tree with a very bushy top, to enjoy the shade and quench their thirst from the jars of cool water set round the foot of the tree.

An officer noted that there were a great many dead and wounded round the tree and also saw that they had been shot from above.

> The officer called to a soldier to look if he could see anyone in the tree-top. The soldier had his rifle loaded and stepping back he carefully scanned the top of the trees. He almost immediately called out:
>
> 'I see him sir!'
>
> Cocking his rifle he immediately fired and down fell a body dressed in a tight-fitting red jacket and tight-fitting rose coloured silk trousers; and the breast of the jacket bursting open with the fall showed that the wearer was a woman. She was armed with a pair of heavy old pattern cavalry pistols, one of which was in her belt still loaded and her pouch was still half full of ammunition. From her perch in the tree, which had been carefully prepared before the attack, she had killed more than half a dozen men.

Chapter 12

Remarkable Characters

Amongst the ranks of the Highlanders, as well as amongst their officers, there were very many remarkable characters at one time or another. It is difficult to pick out any who were particularly outstanding without inevitably overlooking many with equal, or possibly greater, claims to fame. The following for one reason or another were in their ways exceptional, and seem worthy of note.

Mr. Malcolm Macpherson of Phoiness joined Prince Charles and fought by his side at Culloden, when aged fifty-seven. In his view the Highlanders were only defeated then because the French had treacherously betrayed them by not standing by their promises of support. After a long and, as it turned out, ruinous lawsuit he decided in 1757, at the age of seventy, to join Fraser's Highlanders, when they were formed to go over to fight the French in America, in order to get his revenge on them.

He was present with Fraser's Highlanders in 1758 during their seaborne attack on Louisburg commanded by General Wolfe, prior to the attack on Quebec. On two occasions small parties of Fraser's Highlanders were ordered to advance into the brushwood with their broadswords to drive out the sharpshooters lurking there. He

> was particularly noticed for the dexterity and force with which he used his broadsword when his regiment charged the enemy . . . His conduct particularly attracted the notice of General Townshend, who sent for him after the engagement

and, praising his gallant behaviour, expressed surprise how he could leave his native country at such an advanced age to follow the fortune of war. He was so struck with the old man's magnanimity that he took him to England along with him and introduced him to Mr. Pitt. The minister presented him to the King, who was graciously pleased to give him a commission, with leave to return home on full pay.

Mr. Macpherson's family seems to have been a rather remarkable one. A near relation of his, Kenneth Macpherson, who had also been out in the '45 with Prince Charles, similarly found himself penniless. In 1770 he decided to go to India. He was appointed a cadet at an advanced age and eventually attained the rank of Lieutenant-General. He finally died in the year 1815, leaving a considerable fortune to his relatives in Badenoch.

Apart from those whose estates were sequestered, the effects of the rebellion were economically ruinous to many Highlanders, regardless of which side they had been on. Many were left with little alternative to joining the army, or emigrating, both chiefs and clansmen alike. For instance, when the 74th, or Argyle Highlanders, were formed in 1778, one of their officers was the Chief of the Macquarries, then aged 62.

The last of a long line, which had survived for nearly 600 years, although surrounded by the powerful clans of Macdonalds, Macleans and Campbells, he was finally obliged to sell his property and enter the army. Although in his sixties he was healthy and active and perfectly capable of performing any tasks required of him as a soldier. He fought with the 74th in America and was with them until they were reduced in Stirling on their return to Britain in 1783. He eventually lived to 102, and died without an heir.

Remarkable for sheer size and strength was Sergeant Samuel Macdonald of the 93rd, or Sutherland Highlanders, born in Lairg, Sutherland in 1762. He was six feet ten inches tall with a forty-eight inch chest and proportionately broad frame, and was known, scarcely surprisingly, as 'Big Sam'. He was said to be:

> Extremely strongly built and muscular, but yet proportional, unless his legs might be thought even too big for the load they had to bear. His strength was prodigious but such was his pacific disposition that he was never known to exert it improperly.

At the age of 21 he joined the 1st Foot (The Royal Scots) and served with them as Fugleman for six years. While in London he acted as Hercules in a classical play at the Drury Lane Theatre, and for two years he was employed as a lodge porter at Carlton House by the Prince of Wales. In 1792 he joined the Sutherland Fencibles and was promoted to Sergeant in the Colonel's Company. While in the Fencibles the Duchess of Sutherland allowed him 2/6d a day extra pay as she considered: 'so large a body must require more sustenance than his military pay could afford.'

On the formation of the 93rd, or Sutherland Highlanders, in 1799 he was promptly attested and promoted Sergeant, remaining as Supernumary Sergeant in the Colonel's Company. He was considered too big to go in the ranks so he stood on the right of the regiment in line and headed it in column. On the march he was accompanied by his pet, a red deer of uncommon size. A private in the same company, named Mackay, who was 6 feet 2 inches tall and also a powerful man, marched with him at the head of the regiment 'to clear the road'.

Inevitably, with such a man, innumerable stories were told of his feats of strength, but, as indicated, he never misused it. Like many large men he was of exceedingly mild disposition and this, combined with the mild and clear way he gave his instructions made him an excellent drill instructor. He also seems to have been entrusted with the catering for his company when the 93rd were stationed in Dublin. On one occasion when he was buying meat for them at a butcher two miles from the Richmond barracks, he demonstrated his powers. The butcher, thinking to set him an impossible task, challenged him to carry a bullock's carcase to the barracks, saying:

'If you carry it to Richmond you shall have it for nothing.'

Sam thereupon 'got the carcase on his back and to the astonishment of the chopfallen butcher succeeded in carrying it triumphantly to the barracks'.

When wearing full regimentals, kilt, bonnet and feathers, he appeared, of course, an enormous figure, extremely conspicuous in the streets, both in Dublin and Edinburgh. Occasionally his good nature was taken advantage of and though he seldom resented tricks played on him he was sometimes known to get his own back. A cab driver in Edinburgh had a habit of flicking at him with his whip in passing and this finally proved too much for Sam. He turned round and seized hold of the back of the cab, effectively stopping the horse. In spite of the cab driver's efforts in whipping the wretched beast Sam held the cab firmly at a halt until the man came at his command and begged pardon on his knees, to the great amusement of the spectators.

Not so amusing was another occasion in Dublin, when some medical students, who wanted to examine his body in the nude, invited him into a public house ostensibly just for a drink. After several drinks they broached their suggestion that he should strip for their examination, offering him a sum of money to do so. On his refusal to consider the idea they threw themselves on him and attempted to strip him forcibly. This was more than even he could stand. Using one of them as a club he soon cleared the room and threw them downstairs.

While this rough-house was going on, a crowd gathered round the front door, vociferous in condemning the Scottish giant who dared to manhandle honest Irish boys. The house was soon besieged and as Sam went outside a blacksmith hit him a violent blow on the head from behind with his smithy hammer. Fortunately Sam was wearing his feathered bonnet, which absorbed most of the blow, although even so it nearly stunned him. Recovering himself quickly he forced his way through the crowd without difficulty. It is said that the mark of the blow, which would have killed any ordinary man, remained on his head until his death and may even have contributed to his early demise, aged 41, four years later. He was buried in St. Peter Port, Guernsey, in the Stranger's Cemetery, on the 9th of May, 1802.

The history of the 92nd, or Gordon Highlanders, includes a brief mention of a Private Donald Cameron, known as Donald Mor Og, from Lochaber, who was probably one of their strongest men. He came from a fighting family, for his father, Donald Mor Cameron, carried Lochiel's standard at Prestonpans. On crossing the moss which existed there then the men got out of order and Lochiel ordered them to halt and dress their ranks, whereupon Donald Mor cried out:

'The devil a halt and dress there will be today. Let the men go on while their blood is up!'

'God bless you, let it be as you say,' replied Lochiel, and the clan rushed on to victory.

At the famous landing in Aboukir Bay in 1801 Private Donald Cameron was attacked by a French dragoon. Donald parried the Frenchman's blow, transfixing the man with his bayonet and lifting him clean out of the saddle, threw him over his shoulder, shouting at the same time:

'There, men! There's a blow for Abercromby!'

When Donald left the regiment he was often visited by

the Duke of Gordon, who as Marquis of Huntly had been his Colonel, whenever the latter was passing through his Lochaber estates. He would treat the Duke with the respectful familiarity, which was characteristic of the old-fashioned Highlander, pressing on him the best his cottage could afford. Donald was a good deer-stalker and as shootings were not let then the Duke did not worry about him helping himself to the deer, though no doubt he found it tame work after transfixing Frenchmen at Aboukir.

Mention of Aboukir inevitably brings to mind Sir Ralph Abercromby, a remarkable member of an even more remarkable family. General Abercromby had seen little service, except as a subaltern of dragoons, for a short time in Germany during the Seven Years War. It was only at the age of 61 that he first took the field in 1793 as a General in an active campaign.

> He had a strong and vigorous intellect with a military genius, which overcame the disadvantages of inexperience . . . At this age, when many men are retiring from the fatigues of life, he commenced an honourable and successful career of military duty. From the very outset he displayed great talent.

General Stewart, who knew them well wrote:

> There was something remarkable in this family. The father who was born in 1704 lived to see his four sons honoured and respected and at the head of their different professions. While his eldest son, Sir Ralph was Commander in Chief in the West Indies, his second son, Sir Robert, held the same station in the East; Lord Abercromby the third son, was an eminent, learned and virtuous judge; and the fourth died in possession of an independent fortune acquired in the service of the East India Company. Three of his daughters married gentleman of family and fortune, who resided so near him he could dine with either any day he chose; and his fourth daughter continuing unmarried devoted her days to the declining years of her

father. Latterly he lived with his son. I happened to be in Edinburgh in May 1800 and dined with Lady Abercromby on the day Sir Ralph left her to embark on that expedition (to Egypt) from which he never returned. A King's Messenger had arrived from London the day before and Sir Ralph, only waiting for a few family arrangements, set out the following morning. When at dinner after his departure, I was affected in a manner which I can never forget by the respectable old gentleman's anxiety about his son and his observations and inquiries about his future intentions and what service was intended for him. His particular destination was not known, but it was suspected he would be immediately employed.

'They will wear him out,' said he, 'too soon,' (the son was then in his 68th year) 'and make an old man of him before his time with their expeditions to Holland one year and the West Indies the next; and if he would follow my advice he would settle at home and take his rest.'

And when Lady Abercromby observed that she was afraid he must go abroad, 'Then,' said he, 'he will never see me more.'

The verification of this melancholy prediction was to be expected from his great age, being then in his 97th year. He died in the month of July following, eight months before his son, whose absence he regretted so much.

Sir Ralph Abercromby himself, as we have seen, was successful at Aboukir and in the battle of Alexandria, where in Private Dowie's words, he was 'cutting behind and before just like a youth of twenty'. Nor did he mention the fact that he had a musket ball lodged in his hip until the battle was over and victory had been won. He died a week later. His body was placed in a hogshead of rum to be taken home for burial in England, but the barrel leaked and he was buried instead in the fort at the mouth of Valetta harbour in Malta.

In a history of the 93rd, or Sutherland Highlanders, there is a mention of a Private John Mackay, a man of mordant wit, who became a champion boxer in the regiment. He had no interest in boxing until he and some friends were in a public house in 1805 when the 93rd were stationed in Ireland. A local Irish bully, a giant of a man entered and challenged any of the Scots to a bout of fisticuffs. They replied that they had not come to Ireland to fight and that anyway they knew nothing of fisticuffs. This pacific reply merely encouraged him and he challenged the best man in their regiment on any terms. This finally made John Mackay angry and he agreed to fight the man.

A space was cleared and the Irishman set himself in an attitude of self-defence. John who was a small man, but light on his feet, eyed his large opponent from a distance, then suddenly launched himself head-first into the Irishman's stomach. The unexpected attack laid the Irishman senseless. The Highlanders then drew their bayonets and cleared the house. Thereafter John decided to learn to box.

In 1815, at the battle of New Orleans, a cannon-ball struck his brother's head clean off as he stood beside him and knocked John Mackay down, although leaving him uninjured. He resumed his place in the ranks but soon afterwards a musket-ball shattered his right elbow. The arm was amputated in a field hospital without anaesthetics, as was customary, and he made not a sound during the operation. Then a wounded comrade lying next to him remarked jocularly:

'Well John, you won't be striking anyone with that hand again.'

John appeared to ignore this remark and instead addressed the surgeon politely:

'May I just have a last look at that hand which has served me so long and so well?'

The surgeon obligingly passed it to him and he took a last long look at it before reaching across and striking his neighbour a sharp blow on the head with it, saying at the same time:

'You will be the last.'

He returned to Strathnaver in time to be evicted and lived for a further fifty years in the parish of Farr enjoying his pension of 6d a day. He finally died in 1865.

The Highlanders seem to have had remarkable strength and endurance, both officers and men. Captain 'Black Hugh' Fraser of the 93rd Highlanders gave a demonstration of his in Bridgetown, the capital of Barbados when the regiment was stationed in the West Indies in 1825. He was a large and powerful man and in one of the principal shops kept by a Jew he one day noticed some sacks lying on the counter.

'What is in those sacks?' he inquired of the owner.

'Doubloons,' replied the Jew. 'Now you are a very strong man, Captain Fraser, and if you can carry those two sacks to St. Anne's barracks without putting them down you shall have the contents.'

'Done,' said Fraser, promptly.

The sacks were hoisted on to his back and to the increasing horror and distress of the shopowner he marched directly to the barracks without once stopping on the way. Finally, as he entered the gates of the barracks, the wretched merchant burst into tears as he saw his doubloons vanishing, as he imagined, for ever. However, Fraser, having taught him never to underestimate the strength of a Highlander again, was quite content and after keeping the doubloons in his quarters for some time returned them to their owner.

A brief account of the life of Major-General MacBean, V.C., who won his coveted decoration at the Siege of Lucknow, is of interest. He was born of poor parents in Inverness in 1818 and began life as a labourer. He enlisted in the 93rd in 1835 and by 1852 had reached the rank of Colour Sergeant. He was not present at the battle of Alma, having been put in charge of the baggage and only arrived in the Crimea in 1854, but in 1854 he became a Lieutenant and was appointed Adjutant in 1855.

Surgeon General Munro recounted his exploits at Lucknow:

> After entering the breach, one of our officers (MacBean) as brave a man as ever lived and yet as simple as a child, found himself almost alone surrounded by the enemy. But he wielded his sword so dexterously and made such good use of his revolver, that after a desperate struggle in which he killed eleven of his foes he stood unharmed. Some time afterwards a regimental parade was held for the purpose of presenting his well earned Victoria Cross and as the General, Sir R. Garnett, pinned the decoration on his breast, he addressed him in the following words:
>
> 'This cross has been awarded to you for the conspicuous gallantry you displayed at the assault of the enemy's position at Lucknow, on which occasion you killed eleven of the enemy by whom you were surrounded. And a good day's work it was, Sir!'
>
> 'Tuts,' said my gallant and simple friend, quite forgetting that he was on parade and perhaps a little piqued at his performance being spoken of as a day's work. 'Tuts, it didn'a tak twenty minutes.'

The gallant MacBean received a brevet majority with his Victoria Cross and became a Captain in 1858. In 1872 he became a Major and brevet Lieutenant-Colonel. Finally, in 1877 he became a brevet Colonel and in 1878 a Major-General. Having then reached the age of sixty he was retired on a pension of £420, along with a good service pension of £100. As Major-General MacBean, V.C., he had come a long way from the simple Highland labourer of his youth.

Chapter 13

Exceptional Battles

Amongst the many occasions when the Highland regiments were in action around the world, it is invidious to make any special selections, but certain occasions were obviously particularly notable. All those chosen are examples of the Highlander's courage and tenacity, and generally a Highland brigade, or more than one Highland regiment, was involved. For one reason or another each of these battles has its special points of interest for Highland regiments.

The most successful major amphibious combined operation in which the Highlanders were engaged was the landing at Aboukir in 1801, which heralded the end of Napoleon's ambitions in the Near East. The British forces were under the command of Lieutenant-General Sir Ralph Abercromby. With only 15,330 men he faced double the number of French troops, entrenched in the sandhills of Aboukir Bay and supported by artillery as well as strong forces of cavalry and infantry, based on the stronghold of Aboukir itself. The cannon of Fort Aboukir were so placed as to be able to bring a heavy cross-fire to bear on any approach, and they were supported by concealed mortars strategically placed nearby. The French considered it impregnable.

At around two in the morning of January 8th, the 42nd, 79th and 92nd Highlanders were part of a force of 5,230 troops manning the ships' boats, provided by the Navy, off Aboukir Bay. It took nearly seven hours' preparation to arrange them correctly, but by nine o'clock the entire force, in exact order of battle, was being rowed towards the shore, the soldiers packed in silence, in light marching order, with loaded muskets between their legs. The sea began to boil as cannon and mortars opened fire and grape, round-shot and shells showered the water. Three boats, each containing sixty men, were sunk within a hundred yards of the land. Many were saved, but inevitably the wounded were drowned. Counter-fire was provided by light armed vessels and bomb-ketches and gun-brigs moored broadside to the beach, but with little effect against the enemy's fire. Undaunted, the sailors pulled steadily for the shore and soon a hail of musketry fire was added to the hostile cannonade. Then the troops leaped into the surf, forming line as they gained the beach with fixed bayonets and colours flying, while loud cheers rang from flank to flank.

> The Royal Highlanders on the right centre leaped ashore, formed on the beach and rushing up the steep ascent, rendered difficult by the loose sand, in the face of the fire of a battalion of infantry and two guns, speedily gained the summit and instantly closing on their numerous opponents with the bayonet drove them from their position before they had time to fire a second volley.

It is said that after the regiment had formed in line the command 'Fix Bayonets' was given. This was followed by the customary 'Prime and Load'. Then a voice from the rear ranks, later traced to Private Donald Black, an old smuggler from Skye, was heard to shout:

'No prime and load—but charge baignets—immediately!'

Thereupon the entire regiment charged as one man, ascended the heights at the double and carried the position with cold steel.

Scarcely had the Royal Highlanders driven back the French infantry when a squadron of cavalry galloped forward to charge them, but it was immediately repulsed with the loss of its commanding officer. The French then rallied in the rear of a second line of sandhills, from which they maintained a straggling fire, but the British troops pressed on and soon drove them from the field. They thus achieved a victory 'almost without parallel in the annals of war'. The 42nd had 190 casualties including 31 killed, four-fifths of which were incurred before they reached the crest of the sand-hills.

On their left the 92nd were similarly successful, but with only 140 casualties. When they rallied after their victory the heat of the day and the powder in their mouths from biting off the heads of the cartridges had made them very thirsty. They were greatly relieved to find in the huts recently occupied by the French, not only ample supplies of water, but camp kettles on the fires filled with mutton and poultry, in preparation for the dinner the French had intended having to celebrate their anticipated victory. They made sure it was not wasted.

In February 1815 Napoleon escaped from Elba and returned to France. By March he had been received with open arms in Paris. Europe was once again in a ferment. By May the Black Watch, the Camerons and the Gordon Highlanders had been hastily shipped across to Flanders. During the evening of June 15th each had displayed their skill at the Sword Dance and other Highland dances at the Duchess of Richmond's famous Ball in Brussels, when Wellington received the news of Napoleon's surprise advance and defeat of the allied Prussian forces on the Belgian frontier.

With the rising sun on the glorious June morning of the 16th the Highlanders marched out of the Namur Gate of Brussels bound for the village of Quatre Bras, and were in action in the early afternoon soon after they arrived there. The struggle with Marshal Ney's forces went on for five hours, preventing him from going to Napoleon's aid and from completing the destruction of the Prussian force under Marshal Blücher. All three regiments played a notable part in this impromptu, but decisive battle.

The Black Watch were posted in line on a reverse slope in corn reaching almost shoulder high, covering the cross roads at Quatre Bras. The Brunswick allied cavalry had just passed them, when they returned at speed pursued by French Lancers. There was a brief and nearly fatal delay in recognizing the latter for what they were. Some of the two flank companies were caught before they could form a defensive square and forced to fight in scattered groups. Some of the Lancers succeeded in getting inside the square as it was formed. Savage fighting followed, and the Highlanders suffered heavy casualties before they recovered.

A French cavalry officer, whose horse had been shot under him in the square, found himself crossing swords with a gigantic Black Watch sergeant. Seeing he was no match for the sergeant, the Frenchman called out the only English he knew: 'Quarter, quarter.'

The Highlander, with nearly as little English, shouted back:

'Och, och, inteet, she's no going to cut you in quarters at aal, at aal, but shust in twa halves, inteet.'

Lieutenant-Colonel Macara, the commanding officer, was killed and Captain Archibald Menzies of the Grenadier Company had a miraculous escape. He was six feet six inches tall, and an excellent swordsman as well as a fine figure of a man. Although surrounded by Lancers he slew many of them with his claymore, before at last collapsing from his horse with seventeen wounds in him.

One of the Grenadier Company, Private Donald Mackintosh, was lying mortally wounded close to where Captain Menzies had fallen and where his horse remained standing unattended. A French Lancer approached with the obvious intention of taking the horse, but the dying Highlander could still raise his musket.

'Hoots mon,' he warned. 'Ye maunna tak yon beast. It belongs to oor captain here.'

The Lancer uncomprehendingly seized the horse's bridle and with a supreme effort the private shot him dead and fell back himself. Roused by this interchange the wounded Captain started struggling to his feet and another Lancer, observing this, rode up and leaned forward to give him his death blow. Still undefeated the Captain managed to seize him by the leg and drag him off his horse, grappling with him furiously. Yet another Lancer, seeing the fight, galloped up to thrust his lance into the Captain, but at the last moment Menzies managed to swing his opponent round as a shield, so that he received the thrust instead.

The effect of the blow knocked them both to the ground. There they lay for some minutes, the Frenchman still with his sword in his hand and Menzies expecting any moment to receive his death blow from it. Finally the Frenchman rose and staggered a few paces before falling dead. Then a private from the Grenadier Company appeared and asked the Captain how he was:

'Load your piece and finish me off,' ordered Captain Menzies firmly.

Fortunately, the man was not prepared to accept this order and with the help of another moved his wounded commander to the shelter of the nearby square of the 92nd. Colonel Cameron, commanding officer of the Gordons, was a personal friend of Menzies. He ordered him every attention possible and sent four men to carry him to the rear in a blanket. Not long afterwards Colonel Cameron himself was killed, to the grief of the Gordon Highlanders, but Captain Menzies survived to be promoted to Major and lived, with the scars of seventeen wounds, many years to tell the tale.

The depleted 42nd formed square and repelled attack after attack by the Brigade of Cuirassiers, who had orders to break through the centre. Finally, when reinforcements came, the Cuirassiers were forced to retire. When night-fall came the Black Watch were so reduced that they had to form a single square with the next battalion. Their total loss at Quatre Bras was 298 killed and wounded.

The Cameron casualties at Quatre Bras was 277 killed and wounded.

The 92nd, or Gordon Highlanders, were also engaged all afternoon. Initially they repelled a charge of the Cuirassiers with great success. Later they took part in several successful charges against infantry. Their final charge drove the enemy half a mile down the street and cleared most of the houses in Quatre Bras, but it was then that their commanding officer, Colonel Cameron, was killed. All this was not accomplished without the appallingly high casualty figure of 305 killed and wounded.

Although the Black Watch was not heavily engaged on the 18th at Waterloo, the 79th suffered a further 179 casualties and the 92nd was again involved. An eyewitness account of their famous charge with the Scots Greys, at about three in the afternoon, runs as follows:

> Major General Sir Denis Pack called out ... '92nd—everything has given way on your right and left and you must charge this Column,' upon which he ordered four deep to be formed and closed in to the centre. The Regiment which was then within about 20 yards of the Column fired a volley into them ... The Scots Greys came up at this moment, and doubling round our flanks, and through our centre, where openings were made for them, both Regiments charged together calling 'Vive Scotland for ever,' and the Scots Greys *actually walked over this Column*, and in less than three minutes it was totally destroyed ... one could hardly believe had he not witnessed it that such complete destruction could have been effected in so short a time—some of the French soldiers who were lying wounded were calling out 'Vive L'Empereur,' and others firing their musquets at our men who had advanced past them in pursuit of the flying enemy. The Regiment was then recalled and formed up on its former ground ...

The Gordon Highlanders' casualties at Waterloo were 116 killed and wounded. The Black Watch, not so heavily engaged, had only 5 men killed, 6 officers and 39 rank and file wounded. The six officers had all been wounded at Quatre Bras.

The 71st, who only arrived in time for Waterloo after marching for thirty-six hours with no halt longer than half an hour and without any food, followed by a night of drenching downpour, were in action the entire day without any respite. They repulsed no less than seven cavalry charges and at one time sheltered the Duke of Wellington himself in their square. Finally, they charged and sent the Imperial Guard staggering into disorder. Scarcely surprisingly, their casualties were no less than 211 killed and wounded. The 2nd battalion of the 73rd, also heavily involved all day, had even heavier casualties, with 330 killed or wounded and only one officer out of 23 left on his feet at the finish. Once again, the Highlanders had maintained their high reputation as fighting troops to be relied on at all times and in all circumstances.

No record of exceptional battles in which the Highland regiments were engaged would be complete without mention of the Crimean War. In 1854 at Scutari in the Crimea the 42nd, or Black Watch, the 79th, or Cameron Highlanders, and 93rd, or Sutherland Highlanders were brigaded together as a single Highland Brigade under General Sir Colin Campbell, later Lord Clyde. At the battle of Alma on the 20th of September 1854 the Highland Brigade, with its three Highland battalions under Sir Colin Campbell were given the task of protecting the left flank of the British army. They not only overcame and put to flight eight Russian battalions, the pick of the Russian army, but caused four more to retreat.

Before his brigade had moved from column into line before the battle Sir Colin addressed them as follows:

> Now men. You are going into action. Remember this; whoever is wounded—no matter what his rank—must lie where he falls till the bandsmen come to attend to him. No soldiers must go carrying off wounded comrades. If any man does such a thing his name shall be stuck up in his parish church. The army will be watching you; make me proud of the Highland Brigade!

When the time came for action he rode to the head of the Black Watch and gave the command: 'Forward 42nd.'

With his staff he rode rapidly in advance to the top of the crest ahead. To his immediate front lay a deep and broad depression, on the further side of which the Kazan column of two battalions faced him, on the left of which was re-forming the right Vladimir column, which had been forced to retreat by the Guards on their flank. Both columns had suffered casualties, but still numbered 3,000 against the 830 of the 42nd.

When Sir Colin looked to his left he saw on the left of the hollow another and heavier column consisting of two perfectly fresh battalions of the Sousdal Regiment. However, they were stationary, and in spite of the fact that the men were out of breath, Sir Colin sent the 42nd, firing as it advanced, straight across the hollow at the Kazan and Vladimir battalions. The 42nd had not advanced far when the Sousdal column on the left was seen advancing towards the left flank of the 42nd.

Sir Colin halted the 42nd and was about to throw back its left wing to meet this threat, when he saw the 93rd, or Sutherland Highlanders, had reached the crest. In its eagerness to get at the enemy its formation had suffered a little. Sir Colin rode in front of it, re-formed it under fire, and then led it forward against the flank of the Sousdal column, while the 42nd continued their attack on the Vladimir and Kazan columns.

Before the attack of the two Highland regiments the

Russian columns were staggering, and their officers manifestly had extreme difficulty in compelling their men to retain their formation. Then, from the upper ground on the left, yet another Russian column, the right Sousdal column, was seen advancing for the flank of the 93rd. Fortunately, at that instant the 79th, or Cameron Highlanders, came bounding forward and the Sousdal column was 'taken in the flagrant offence of daring to march across the front of a British battalion advancing in line'. After a moment's halt to dress their ranks the Cameron men sprang at the flank of the Sousdal column and shattered it with a fierce fire poured into its close-packed ranks. At the same instant the left Sousdal column, beaten back by the 93rd, and the Kazan and Vladimir columns assailed by the Black Watch, turned in full retreat. The hill spurs and hollows were thronged with disordered ranks of retreating Russians. The shrill strains of the pipes in full blast and the nodding plumes of the Highlanders and waving tartans of the kilts had overcome enormous odds.

Sir Colin halted his brigade and held them on the ground they had won. The Ouglitz column, 4,000 strong and still fresh, advanced from its height, intending to check the retreat and force the flying columns to turn back into action. But they too in their turn gave way before the fire of the Highland Brigade and retreated slowly, covering their defeated countrymen. No less than twelve battalions of the élite of the Czar's troops of the line had been defeated by the Highlanders in the two-deep British line formation.

This was indeed a magnificent victory, but the Crimea was the scene of other famous Highland actions, as well. Let Surgeon General William Munro, who was with the 93rd Highlanders at the time, describe the battle of Balaclava on October 25th in his own words:

> A considerable body of horse wheeling south advanced in our direction at a brisk pace, which gradually increased to a

gallop. While they were approaching, Sir Colin Campbell ordered the 93rd and the battalions of Turkish troops on either flank to re-form line on the crest of the hill; and as we were doing so, the two Companies of the Regiment, which had been detached under the command of Major Gordon, arrived and took up their position in the line. Thus we stood for a few seconds, while the cavalry were rapidly nearing us; but the Turkish battalions on our flanks began to get unsteady and at last fairly turned, broke and bolted. It was at this moment that Sir Colin rode along the front of the 93rd telling the Regiment to be 'Steady!' for if necessary every man would have 'to die where he stood.' He was answered by the universal and cheery response, 'Ay, ay, Sir Colin, need's be we'll do that.'

I write exactly what I saw and heard. The men of the 93rd were in excellent spirits, burning to fight; and I do not think there was a single soldier standing in the line who had an anxious thought as to our isolated and critical position, or who for a moment felt the slightest inclination to flinch before the charge of the advancing cavalry. On the contrary they appeared to have settled themselves firmly where they stood to receive the expected shock and to be pleased that everything depended on themselves in what they expected was to be a regular hand to hand struggle.

When Sir Colin thought our Minié rifles might reach the enemy, he ordered the line to fire a volley; but, when the smoke from this had blowu aside, we saw the cavalry was still advancing straight for the line. A second volley rang forth, and then we observed that there was a little confusion in the enemy's ranks and that they were swerving to our right.

The men of the 93rd at that moment became a little, just a little, restive and brought their rifles to the charge, manifesting an inclination to advance and meet the cavalry half-way with the bayonet. But old Sir Colin brought them sharply back to discipline. He could be angry, could Sir Colin, and when in an angry mood spoke sharply and quick, and when very angry was given to use *emphatic* language; and such he made use of on that occasion. The men were quiet and steady in a moment and then the grenadiers, under my old friend Ross, were ordered to change front and fire a volley. This third volley was at a much nearer range than the previous ones and caught the cavalry in the flank as they were approaching, apparently with the intention of passing by our right. It shook them visibly and caused them to bend away to their own left until they had completely wheeled, when they rode back to their own army, followed by a burst of wild cheering from the ranks of the 93rd, which from that day has been spoken of as the 'Thin Red Line,' and is the only infantry regiment which bears upon its colours the word 'Balaklava.'

11. Sgt 'Big Sam' Macdonald of the 93rd

12. Piper Kenneth Mackay of the 79th Cameron Highlanders at Waterloo

13. Pipe Major John MacDonald of the 72nd Highlanders, 1854

14. Pipe Major Duncan Smith of the 92nd Highlanders, *circa* 1820

15. The Black Watch attacked by Indians at Bushy Run, 1763

16. The 75th Gordon Highlanders at the storming of Seringapatam, 1799

17. The Black Watch hurl the French back at Corunna, 1809

18. The charge of the Gordons and Royal Scots Greys at Waterloo

19. The Highland Brigade at the Battle of the Alma, 1854

20. The Black Watch repel the Russians at Sebastopol, 1855

21. 'The thin red streak, tipped with a line of steel'. The 93rd at Balaclava, 25 October, 1854

22. Men of the 71st Highland Light Infantry in the Crimea

23. The 78th Highlanders at Lucknow, 25 September, 1857

Chapter 14

In North America

The first Highland regiments to land in North America in 1757 to fight the French were the 42nd Royal Highland Regiment, or Black Watch, the 77th, or Montgomerie's Highlanders and the 78th, or Fraser's Highlanders. A historian noted:

> When the Highland regiments landed in that continent their garb and appearance attracted much notice. The Indians in particular were delighted to see a European regiment in a dress so similar to their own. A New Yorker wrote: When the Highlanders landed they were caressed by all ranks and orders of men, but more particularly by the Indians. On the march to Albany, the Indians flocked from all quarters to see the strangers who, they believed, were of the same extraction as themselves, and therefore received them as brothers.

The Highlanders soon proved they had more in common with the Indians than a superficial resemblance in dress. Their woodcraft also proved superior to the ordinary, accustomed as they were to stalking deer in their native hills. In a letter home an English general wrote:

> The Highlanders seem particularly calculated for this country and species of warfare, requiring great personal exertion; their patience, sober habits and hardihood—their bravery, their agility and their dress contribute to adapt them to this climate and render them formidable to the enemy.

The Highlanders also proved themselves good shots and it was noted: 'that although debarred the use of arms in their own country, they showed themselves good marksmen, and had not forgotten how to handle their arms.' The old trick with the bonnet also proved useful once again when the 42nd were making a foraging expedition in the Jerseys in 1758:

> In the excursion through the woods, a Highlander came unexpectedly in sight of an American, when their pieces happened to be unloaded. Each flew behind a tree to cover himself while loading, but fearing that the first who ventured out of cover would be brought down by the other, both kept possession of their trees, till at last the Highlander, losing patience, pushed his bonnet beyond the tree on the point of his bayonet. The American shot his ball through its centre, when his opponent starting forward made him surrender instantly.

Inevitably, some of the Highlanders were captured by the Indians, for the French relied a great deal upon their Indian allies. A private in the 77th, or Montgomerie's Highlanders, managed to avoid being tortured and outwitted his Indian captors in an unusual way:

> Several soldiers of this and other regiments fell into the hands of the Indians, being taken in an ambush. Allan Macpherson, one of these soldiers, witnessing the miserable fate of several of his fellow prisoners, who had been tortured to death by the Indians, and seeing them preparing to commence the same operations on himself, made signs that he had something to communicate. An interpreter was brought. Macpherson told them, that provided his life was spared for a few minutes, he would communicate the secret of an extraordinary medicine, which, if applied to the skin, would cause it to resist the strongest blow of a tomahawk, or sword, and that, if they would allow him to go to the woods with a guard, to collect the plants proper for his medicine, he would prepare it and allow the

experiment to be tried on his own neck by the strongest and most expert warrior amongst them. This story easily gained upon the superstitious credulity of the Indians, and the request of the Highlander was instantly complied with. Being sent into the woods, he soon returned with such plants as he chose to pick up. Having boiled these herbs, he rubbed his neck with their juice and laying his head upon a log of wood, desired the strongest man among them to strike at his neck with his tomahawk, when he would find he could not make the smallest impression. An Indian, levelling a blow with all his might, cut with such force that the head flew off to a distance of several yards. The Indians were fixed in amazement at their own credulity, and the address with which their prisoner had escaped the lingering death prepared for him; but, instead of being enraged at the escape of their victim, they were so pleased with his ingenuity, that they refrained from inflicting further cruelties on the remaining prisoners.

The Highlanders played their part in the warfare in Canada and Newfoundland at the capture of Quebec, Montreal and St. Johns, among many other notable occasions. Following the end of the Seven Years War with France in 1763 they found themselves involved in quelling a full-scale uprising of the Cherokee Indians. In this, also, they proved successful.

Typical of the warfare against the Indians was the difficulty of bringing them into the open. When the 42nd Royal Highland Regiment, together with some of the 77th, or Montgomerie's Highlanders and some of the 60th Regiment were detailed to guard a column of supplies destined for Fort Pitt in 1763, they were ambushed by Indians in a steep-sided pass at Bushy Run. The column was surrounded, but whenever they sallied out to attack the Indians retreated. Finally two companies were ordered to feign a retreat. This enticed the Indians to attack, whereupon two more companies doubled round a hill and attacked them on the flank. In the ensuing action the Indians were so severely mauled that the column was able to press on to Fort Pitt without further trouble.

The Highlanders seem to have been popular in America. The *Virginia Gazette* for 30th July, 1767 reads with obvious sincerity:

> Last Sunday evening the Royal Highland Regiment embarked for Ireland which regiment since its arrival in America has been distinguished for having undergone most amazing fatigues, made long and frequent marches through an unhospitable country, bearing excessive heat and severe cold with an alacrity and cheerfulness, frequently encamping in deep snow ... continually exposed in camp and on their marches to the alarms of a savage enemy, who in all their attempts were forced to fly ... The freemen of this and the neighbouring provinces have most sincerely to thank them for that resolution and bravery with which they ... defeated the enemy and insured us peace and security from a savage foe; and ... they have our thanks for that decorum in behaviour which they maintained during their stay in this city ...

With the outbreak of the War of Independence in 1776 the Highlanders returned to America. The experiences of the 71st, or Fraser's Highlanders were perhaps typical of this period. They acquitted themselves well at the battle of Brooklyn and the siege of Savannah, to quote only two occasions. Finally, like Macdonald's Highlanders, they were made prisoner when General Cornwallis capitulated at Yorktown, but, as with Macdonald's Highlanders, not a man of the 71st would violate his oath of allegiance in spite of all the inducements held out to them to do so.

Occasionally they found themselves opposed to those they had known well in previous years. An instance of this was mentioned in the history of the 71st:

> During the skirmishing warfare in the Jerseys and Pennsylvania in the years 1776 and 1777, Lieutenant Colonel

Maitland, son of the Earl of Lauderdale, was particularly active. Ever on the alert, and having his Highlanders always ready, he attracted the particular notice of General Washington. Some communications having passed between them as old acquaintances, although then opposed as enemies, Colonel Maitland sent intimation to the American commander, that in future his men would be distinguished by a red feather in their bonnets, so that he could not mistake them, nor avoid doing justice to their exploits, in annoying his posts, and obstructing his convoys and detachments; adding that General Washington was too liberal not to acknowledge merit, even in an enemy. Fraser's Highlanders wore the red feather after Colonel Maitland's death and continued to do so till the conclusion of the war.

(When peace was signed in 1783 the 71st was reduced, but General Stewart noted: 'In the year 1795 the red feather was assumed by the Royal Highland Regiment.')

Perhaps typical of much of the fighting in the American War of Independence was the following account of the battle of Pisquita in 1777:

On the afternoon of May 10th the American Generals Maxwell and Stephens attacked the Royal Highlanders in Pisquita with 2,000 men. Advancing with secrecy and favoured by the ground, their approach was unperceived till they suddenly rushed on to a level space in front of the Highland picquets. The attack was so unexpected that the men had scarcely time to sieze their arms, but they kept the enemy in check till the reserve picquet came up. Pushing on in strength the enemy mixed with the picquets, who retired disputing every step to gain time for the regiment to turn out. Thus time to assemble was obtained and the enemy were driven back with great precipitation, leaving upwards of 200 men killed and wounded. The Highlanders pursuing ardently were only prevented by nightfall from pushing on to attack the hostile camp. The loss of the Highlanders was but three sergeants and nine privates killed; Captain Duncan Macpherson, Lieutenant

> William Stewart, three sergeants and thirty privates wounded . . . (but) The fighting in this skirmish was very bitter, most of it being at close quarters. Lt. Stewart and three sergeants were disabled for life, as well as many of the men. The loss of six sergeants, all men of the best conduct and character, was counted as a serious one to the regiment.

Even so the battle had its lighter moments:

> When the picquet was overpowered Sergeant Macgregor was severely wounded and left insensible on the ground. The sergeant had that day put on a new jacket with silver lace and large silver buckles on his shoes; and he attracted the notice of an American soldier, who reckoned him a good prize. The retreat of the sergeant's comrades not allowing the American time to strip the Scotsman on the spot, he took him on his back to a more convenient distance. By this time Macgregor began to recover, and perceiving whither the American was carrying him, he drew his dirk, grasped the other by the throat and swore he would run him through if he did not turn back and carry him to the camp. The American finding this argument irresistible, complied with the demand, and meeting Lord Cornwallis and Colonel Stirling, was thanked for his care of the sergeant; but he honestly told them that he was only carrying the Scottish sergeant to camp because he wished to save his own life. Lord Cornwallis gave the American his liberty and procured for Sergeant Macgregor a billet under Government.

It is notable that 'upwards of 300' of the old 78th, or Fraser's Highlanders, who had previously served in Canada and Nova Scotia and settled there in 1763 after the war with France, now formed the nucleus of the two battalions of the 84th or Royal Highland Emigrant Regiment embodied in 1775, although not regimented or numbered until 1778. They were instrumental in defending Quebec in 1776 and were also in many other actions.

> Their uniform was the full Highland garb, with purses made of racoons' instead of badgers' skins. The officers wore the broad sword and dirk, and the men a half basket sword. At the conclusion of the war both were reduced and grants of land given to the officers and men ... All those who had been settled in America previously to the war, remained.

The officers of the Royal Highland Emigrant Regiment were involved on one occasion in a strange little contretemps, as follows:

> On St. Andrew's day a ball was given by the officers of the garrison in which they were quartered, to the ladies in the vicinity. When one of the ladies entered the ballroom and saw the officers in the Highland garb, her sensitive delicacy revolted at what she thought an indecency, declaring she would quit the room if these were to be her company. This occasioned some little embarrassment. An Indian lady, sister of the Chief Joseph Brandt, who was present with her daughters, observing the bustle, inquired what was the matter, and, being informed, she cried out:
>
> 'This must be a very indelicate lady to think of such a thing. She shows her own arms and elbows to all the men, and she pretends she cannot look at these officer's bare legs, although she will look at my husband's bare thighs for hours together; she must think of other things, or she would see no more shame in a man showing his legs, than she does in showing her own neck and breast.'
>
> These remarks turned the laugh against the lady's squeamish delicacy and the ball was permitted to proceed without the officers being obliged to retire.

Not all the emigrant Highlanders in America joined the 84th. In 1781 a settlement of emigrant Highlanders at Cross Creek, who had been consistently loyal to the British side from the start of the war, offered to raise 1,500 men, finding their own clothing and subsistence and only requiring arms and ammunition. For some strange reason this offer was not accepted and they mostly returned to their settlement when the British army marched for Wilmington.

General Stewart recorded an exception:

> Among these settlers was a gentleman of the name of Macneil, who had been an officer in the Seven Years War. He joined the army with several followers, but soon took his leave, having been rather sharply reprimanded for his treatment of a republican family. He was a man of tall stature and commanding aspect, and moved, when he walked among his followers, with all the dignity of a chieftain of old. Retaining his loyalty, although offended with the reprimand, he offered to surprise the republican garrison, governor and council assembled at Willisborough. He had three hundred followers, one-half of them old country Highlanders, the other half born in America, and the offspring of Highlanders. The enterprise was conducted with address and the governor, council, and garrison, were secured without bloodshed, and immediately marched off for Wilmington, Macneil and his party travelling by night and concealing themselves in swamps and woods by day. However, the country was alarmed, and a hostile force collected. He proceeded in zig-zag directions, for he had a perfect knowledge of the country, but without any provisions except what chance threw in his way. When he had advanced two-thirds of the route, he found the enemy occupying a pass which he must open by the sword, or perish in the swamps for want of food. At this time he had more prisoners to guard than followers. 'He did not secure his prisoners by putting them to death'; but, leaving them under a guard of half his force on whom he could least depend, he charged with the others sword in hand through the pass and cleared it of the enemy, but was unfortunately killed from too great ardour in the pursuit. The enemy being dispersed, the party continued their march disconsolate for the loss of their leader; but their opponents again assembling in force, the party were obliged to take refuge in the swamps, still retaining their prisoners. The British Commander at Wilmington, hearing of Macneil's enterprise, marched out to his support, and kept firing cannon, in expectation the report would reach them in the swamps. The party heard the

reports; and knowing that the Americans had no artillery, they ventured out of the swamps towards the quarter whence they heard the guns, and meeting with Major (afterwards Sir James) Craig, sent out to support them, delivered over their prisoners, half famished with hunger, and lodged them safely in Wilmington. Such partisans as these are invaluable in active warfare.

With the end of the War of Independence in 1783 the Highlanders saw no more fighting in North America for thirty years. In 1813 the Americans, exasperated by the blockade of shipping, declared war on the British. In 1814 the war in Europe ended with Napoleon's abdication after the battle of Toulouse. The 93rd Sutherland Highlanders, returned to England in August after garrisoning the Cape of Good Hope for nine years, were shipped in September to America as part of an ill-conceived expedition to descend on the American coast. In December they landed near New Orleans, along with the other regiments comprising this expedition.

In January 1815 the 93rd took part in the disastrously mismanaged and badly prepared attack on the extremely well-fortified American position at New Orleans. No scaling ladders were provided, although without them it would have been impossible to cross the broad ditches and high walls of cotton bales, from behind which the well-sheltered American marksmen poured forth a devastatingly accurate and rapid fire. It was a repetition of the slaughter at Ticonderoga, except that the Highlanders were not even allowed to attack.

The 93rd advanced to within 150 yards of the enemy defences when they came under sudden, extremely accurate and heavy fire. They continued to advance undaunted until very close to the wall of the enemy fortification, when for no obvious reason they were peremptorily halted. They stood fast under the galling fire and endured appalling casualties of 607 officers and men, or 75 per cent of their strength killed, wounded or missing. The Americans had only 13 killed, 39 wounded and 71 missing.

The daughter of an American who was present wrote:

> I have often heard my father say that both officers and men (of the 93rd) gave proof of the most intrepid gallantry and that it moved him to tears as he saw man after man of magnificent Highlanders mowed down by the murderous artillery and rifle fire. They moved forward in perfect order, giving three cheers as they advanced, heedless of the pitiless storm of balls, and only gave way when 50 per cent of their number lay dying on the field. A little drummer boy climbed up a tree and continued to cheer the poor fellows on until the end of the fight.

An American officer, an eyewitness, observed afterwards:

> Whatever was the name of that regiment (the 93rd) they were the most surprising instance of cool determined bravery and undaunted courage I ever heard of, standing in the midst of a most destructive fire, firm and immovable as a brick wall.

Less than ten days after this mismanaged and bungled affair at New Orleans news was received that peace had been declared. Many of the wounded pensioners from that 'brick wall' arrived home in Sutherland only to be evicted, or in some cases to find their homes burned to the ground. Small wonder that some were heard to declare: 'If we had arms and ammunition in our hands, tired, weary and crippled as we are, we would march to Dunrobin Castle (the Duke of Sutherland's home) and level it to the ground in less time than we stood at New Orleans to be shot at by the Yankees!' Nor was it surprising that recruiting became difficult, or that the flow of emigrants to America increased.

It was a further twenty-four years before the Highlanders again found themselves fighting in North America. In 1837 discontent with the economic conditions in Upper and Lower Canada compared with the more progressive United States, led to a conspiracy to throw off British rule. The insurgents, mostly French Canadians, took possession of Navy Island, a little above Niagara Falls, and were supplied by a steamboat named *The Carolina*, ferrying ammunition from the United States. The steamboat was captured and set on fire, then allowed to drift over the Falls. The rebels were defeated and dispersed, and although the ringleaders managed to escape, some of the prisoners captured were executed. This led to a flare-up of the rebellion in 1838.

In late October 1838 the 93rd arrived in Quebec. In freezing November conditions they were embarked on crowded steamers and forced to remain on deck all night with only their greatcoats as protection. Disembarked at Ontario, they marched and counter-marched on roads knee-deep in snow and mud. Finally they cornered the rebels in a windmill and 159 rebels, including 131 American citizens, surrendered.

The officers and men were received with tremendous hospitality by the inhabitants of Toronto and the surrounding district. It was here that the evicted people of Sutherland had found refuge after the Clearances had driven them from their homes. For twenty years previously they had been arriving there, year after year, and they were thus overjoyed to see soldiers of their own country in tartan and kilts. Many of the soldiers were close relations, some sons, others brothers, or cousins of the settlers.

> The delight was mutual, the fraternisation affecting. They recounted all that had happened since they had parted in the dear old land of their birth. They feasted and feted the soldiers, whoever they might be. If they were Sutherland men, all the more endearing, if not, it was enough that they belonged to the Sutherland Regiment, they wore its uniform, which constituted them Sutherland men.

Major Macdonald, Adjutant of the 93rd at this time, wrote:

> In one of the towns we met a Glengarry regiment of Militia hurriedly mustered, and sent to the front. There were some fine strapping men amongst them, but they neither knew anything of discipline nor drill, and moreover scarcely any of them could speak English. I was acting Brigade Major at the time. I had to bring my knowledge of their language (Gaelic) of which I was always proud, to help them along with their drill, and very much pleased the poor fellows were to find that I could give them some instruction and hints in Gaelic. But my efforts did not continue long as the 93rd got orders to move.

The Glengarry Militia referred to were almost certainly Macdonells evicted from Glengarry in Inverness-shire to make way for sheep. The first five hundred were evicted as early as 1782 and settled near Ontario, naming the district itself Glengarry. In 1802 the spendthrift chieftain, Alistair Ranaldson Macdonell of Glengarry, began further massive evictions. These continued throughout his lifetime until 1852. By that time scarcely a clansman remained in Scotland, but something like 10,000 Macdonells lived in Glengarry in Canada. (Earlier in the present century the figure was around 20,000.)

When one considers these figures it is understandable why the Highlanders have generally been sure of a welcome in North America, although there have sometimes been reservations. In 1848, when the 42nd was at Nova Scotia, Lieutenant Chisholm was sent in charge of a detachment to Montreal and attended the great festival at Boston to celebrate the completion of the railway connecting Boston and Montreal. He appeared in full dress and received a tremendous ovation from the Bostonian Scots present. He also attended the grand ball, but could not get any of the Boston young ladies to dance with him, they felt so shy and nervous of the kilt.

Chapter 15

In the Near and Far East

The first Highland regiment to be sent to India, forerunner of many others, was the 1st Battalion of the 73rd, or Macleod's Highlanders. Re-numbered in 1786 as the 71st they were to become famous as the Highland Light Infantry. Raised by Lord Macleod in 1777, they embarked for India in January 1779 and, after surviving the long voyage remarkably well, arrived in January 1780 to find the position of the British in southern India extremely precarious

The forces available to the Honourable East India Company were very weak and the 73rd, as the only all-British regiment, was immediately in action against the French troops acting in conjunction with the Mohammedan adventurer Hyder Ali. In September 1780 the 73rd lost their two flank companies, sent to rescue a small force in difficulties against greatly superior numbers. They had successfully relieved it, when their ammunition train blew up leaving them without ammunition against overwhelming numbers. They fought to the last with the bayonet, and the few wounded survivors were thrown into the dungeons of Seringapatam, chained in pairs. Amongst these was Captain David Baird of the 73rd, afterwards General Sir David Baird. Informed of his fate, his mother's only comment was:

'Heaven help the lad who's chained to oor Davie!'

The remaining 500 men of the 73rd proved themselves invaluable fighting men. General Sir Eyre Coote relied on them for his victory at Porto Novo against odds of ten to one, 10,000 against 100,000. Afterwards he cherished them as: 'The precious remains of the 73rd Regiment.'

In 1781 the 78th, or Seaforth's Highlanders, raised in 1778, embarked for the East Indies 1,110 rank and file

> all in high health and well disciplined. But however hardy their constitutions and however capable of active exertions on land, they could not withstand the diseases incident on a voyage of eleven months in bad transports and living on food so different from that to which they had been accustomed . . . before they had reached Madras in 1782 230 men had died of scurvy and out of the 1,100 who had sailed from Portsmouth only 390 men were fit to carry arms when they landed . . . they were so reduced by scurvy, night blindness and an accumulation of other diseases that it was six months before they were fit to take the field.

The 73rd Highlanders, the 2nd battalion of the Royal Highlanders, arrived at Bombay on the 5th of March 1782 after a twelve months voyage, having also suffered greatly from scurvy and fever caught on passage. They had lost 121 of all ranks and, like the Seaforth's, were extremely unfit as a result, although able to go into action that year.

All three Highland regiments were soon fighting the French under General Lally and the Indian army under Tippoo Sahib, Hyder Ali's son, who succeeded the latter as Sultan of Mysore on his death. In 1783 the 73rd, 500 strong, with 1,500 native troops, were besieged in Mangalore by an army of 100,000 under Tippoo, directed by French siege experts. Despite the odds, they held out for nine months until offered honourable terms. Then they marched out with all the honours of war and colours flying, although reduced to half their original number.

Peace was signed in 1784, but in 1787 a treaty between France and Holland gave the French the right to garrison Dutch possessions in India. This alarmed the British and encouraged Tippoo. Further trouble was inevitable and the British promptly raised fresh regiments for India, including the 74th Highlanders, who arrived in Madras in 1788. Amongst other young officers commissioned at this time and eager for action was a certain Ensign Arthur Wellesley of the 73rd Highlanders.

In 1789 Tippoo invaded the neighbouring state of Travancore, which the British were bound by treaty to protect. He was defeated, and the Highland regiments again distinguished themselves, but it was not until 1792 that Lord Cornwallis, Governor-General of India, was able to storm Seringapatam itself and force Tippoo to make peace. Finally in 1799 Tippoo again broke the peace and was killed when Seringapatam was stormed by the 74th, led by none other than General Sir David Baird, who had been chained in the dungeons as a Captain. Recognizing some old comrades in the ranks of the 74th, as he prepared to lead the charge, he cried out to them:

'Ah, my lads, now you and I are going to pay off some old scores!'

While various actions continued in India and Ceylon, the British prepared to attack Napoleon's forces in Egypt. In 1801 came the landing at Aboukir Bay. Some three weeks later, on March 21st, the inevitable battle of Alexandria followed. The Highlanders were prominent as ever. The Black Watch was stationed in a ruined palace of the Ptolemies, by the sea, when the attack began in pitch darkness at three in the morning, an hour before dawn. Private Andrew Dowie of the Black Watch gave his account afterwards:

> We warmly engaged a column in front. The morning being very calm and not a breath to carry the smoke away a French regiment passed our right and formed in our rear. This being observed by Major Stirling, who, hearing the officers dressing their line in the French language, instantly ordered the right wing to the right-about, gave them a volley and charged. We

> pushed them forward at the point of the bayonet and in spite of every effort on their part we forced them towards the ruins of Cleopatra's Palace, where they made for a breach in the wall and chocked themselves like cattle forced in at a gate; we were obliged to force forward to get at those inside; by this time it was daybreak; the carnage was dreadful—in fact they were almost annihilated . . . The major then ordered all out of the ruins to support the left wing, which was done as quickly as possible, and commenced firing. The general commanding the French cavalry seeing our irregular formation made a charge at us. Sir Ralph Abercromby seeing the cavalry coming, called us to come to the rear of the tents; in proceeding thither my foot got entangled with a cord . . . During that time I saw Sir Ralph engaged with three of the French cavalry cutting behind and before like a youth of twenty. One of our grenadiers named Barker, having spent his ammunition, charged his piece with loose power from his cartouch, fired his ramrod and killed one of Sir Ralph's assailants, while Sir Ralph struck down another; the third made off. Sir Ralph thanked Barker for having saved his life and asked his name, and when taken to headquarters (he was mortally wounded by a ball in the thigh though he made no comment on the fact until the battle was won) ordered his son to remember Barker.

The Black Watch, Gordon Highlanders and Cameron Highlanders all acquitted themselves well at Alexandria, although the bulk of the fighting and the majority of casualties fell to the first two on that occasion. As a result of the battle the French soon capitulated. Egypt was won and the three Highland regiments acquired a Sphinx in their battle honours.

Amongst the Gordon Highlanders' casualties was their commanding officer, Lieutenant-Colonel Erskine, who was wounded early in the day by grape-shot which mangled his thigh. His leg was amputated, but he died soon afterwards. He was buried, as he had requested, with a gold locket round his neck containing locks of his sister's and his fiancée's hair. In 1894 a soldier in the garrison at Alexandria uncovered a skeleton, minus a leg with a gold locket round its neck. He wrote to *The Times*, and the Gordon Highlanders combined with Colonel Erskine's relatives to have the body suitably re-interred.

Meanwhile, in India, after numerous small actions to round-up the gangs of outlaws formed by the scattered remnants of the Sultan of Mysore's forces, another war broke out. In 1803 the Mahrattas threatened the territory of the Nyzam of Hyderabad, a faithful ally of the British. The 78th under Wellesley, then a Major-General, marched against them and encountered them at the battle of Assaye. Wellesley had a mere 6,000 men, including the 78th, or Seaforth's Highlanders, and the 74th, as his only British infantry. The Mahrattas were 60,000 strong with infantry, cavalry, cannons and European officers.

The 74th were charged on the flank by cavalry and an extremely savage fight ensued. According to one account:

> Captain A. B. Campbell of the 74th, who had on a former occasion lost an arm and afterwards had the remaining arm broken at the wrist by a fall in hunting, was seen in the thickest of the fighting with his bridle in his teeth and the sword in his mutilated hand dealing destruction around him.

In spite of this he seems to have survived the day, although all eighteen officers were cut down.

A regimental historian noted:

> Every officer present ... was either killed or wounded, except Quartermaster James Grant, who, when he saw so many of his friends fall ... though a non-combatant, joined the ranks and fought to the termination of the action.

When Wellesley ordered a general advance and galloped forward to the 74th on his right he found only 40 men instead of 500 and the commanding officer, Lieutenant-Colonel Swinton, was lying in his gore with his back against his dead charger.

'Get the 74th forward, Swinton! Where the devil are the rest of them?'

'They are all down, sir.'

In later years the Duke of Wellington would often relate this story and add how he spent a sleepless night after the victory at Assaye with his head in his hands. The 74th's casualties were 164 officers and men killed, 295 officers and men wounded, of a total of 495, but in spite of these staggering losses the regiment fought on to the end of the Mahratta campaign in 1805. Only two months after Assaye they were engaged in the battle of Argaum, when their losses were, by comparison, a trifling 4 killed and 48 wounded.

Amongst the wounded at Assaye and at Argaum was Lieutenant Langlands. It was recorded:

> A powerful Arab threw a spear at him, and drawing his sword, rushed forward to finish the Lieutenant. But the spear having entered Langlands' leg, cut its way out again and stuck in the ground behind him. Langlands grasped it and, turning the point, threw it with so true an aim that it went right through his opponent's body and transfixed him within three or four yards of his intended victim.

For their services at Assaye the 74th and 78th were granted the unusual honour of a third colour. Known as the Assaye Colour, it was carried by the 74th thereafter. A device, 'The Elephant superscribed Assaye,' was also borne on the regimental colours and incorporated in the regimental badge of the 74th and 78th. In 1805 the 74th returned home after over sixteen years in India, during which their gallant Quartermaster James Grant had seen three sets of officers, nearly all of whom were killed in action. Although it might be imagined they would wish to return home, most of the men who were fit volunteered for other regiments in India.

In 1815 the battle of Waterloo brought peace to Europe, but in India, Africa and the Far East small actions, rebellions, treaty infringements and the policing of unsettled areas, or frontiers, continued to keep the army busy. The Highlanders continued to die from cholera, typhus, malaria and other tropical diseases, as well as bullets. Indeed, during this period the diseases took by far the heavier toll, but there was always the prospect of death in action in some far-flung outpost.

Then came war in the Near East—the Crimea. The Highland brigade was formed under General Sir Colin Campbell and acquitted itself gallantly. The deeds of the 42nd, 79th and 93rd echoed round the world once again, as their gallantry against tremendous odds became known. After the battle of Alma Sir Colin himself wrote:

> Lord Raglan came up presently and sent for me. When I approached him, I observed his eyes to fill and his lips and countenance quiver. He gave me a cordial shake of the hand, but he could not speak. The men cheered very much. I told them I was going to ask the commander-in-chief a great favour —that he would permit me to have the honour of wearing the Highland bonnet during the rest of the campaign, which pleased them very much.

It was recorded:

> The request was at once granted and the making of the bonnet was secretly entrusted to Lieutenant and Adjutant Drysdale of the 42nd. There was the difficulty of how to combine the hackle of the three regiments of the brigade. It was finally decided to have the upper third red for the 42nd and the remaining two thirds white at the bottom for the 79th and 93rd. Only about half a dozen men of the 42nd were concerned in the preparation of the bonnet.
>
> A brigade parade was ordered on the morning of the 22nd September on the battlefield of Alma 'as the General was

desirous of thanking the brigade for its conduct on the 20th.' The square was formed in readiness for the chief's arrival, and he rode into it with the bonnet on. No formal signal was given, but he was greeted with such volumes of cheering that both the English and French armies were startled into wonderment as to what was going on. Such is the history of Sir Colin's feather bonnet.

Sir Colin Campbell's farewell speech to the Highland Brigade in the Crimea is worth quoting:

> Soldiers of the 42nd, 79th and 93rd! Old Highland Brigade! with whom I had passed the early and perilous part of this war. I now have to take leave of you. In a few hours I shall be on board ship never to see you again as a body, a long farewell! I am now old and shall not be called to serve any more, and nothing will remain to me but the memory of my campaign and the enduring, hardy, generous soldiers with whom I have been associated, whose name and glory will long be kept in the hearts of our countrymen. When you go home, as you gradually fulfill your term of service, each to his family and cottage, you will tell the story of your immortal advance in that victorious echelon up the heights of Alma and of the old Brigadier who led and loved you so well. Your children and your children's children will repeat the tale to other generations when only a few lines of history will remain to record all the enthusiasm and discipline which have borne you so stoutly to the end of this war. Our native land will never forget the name of the Highland Brigade and in some future war that native land will call for another one to equal this, which it can never surpass. Though I shall be gone, the thought of you will go with me wherever I may be and cheer my old age with a glorious recollection of danger confronted and hardships endured. A pipe will never sound near me without carrying me back to those bright days when I was at your head and wore the bonnet which you gained for me and the honourable decorations on my breast, many of which I owe to your conduct. Brave soldiers, kind comrades, farewell.

It is understandable that those Highland regiments not sent to the Crimea were eager to have their share in the fighting. The Betting Book of the 78th, or 2nd Battalion Seaforth's Highlanders, has an entry made while stationed at Poona, the well-known Indian hill-station which reads: '5th July 1854: Poona: News having just arrived that the 10th Royal Hussars have just received an order to proceed to Turkey the following officers being of the opinion that it would be decidedly jolly to go with them agree to give the undermentioned quantity of champagne whenever that may occur.' Thirteen signatories guaranteed 66 bottles of champagne.

In the event the 78th never left India, but matters there were approaching a crisis. The mutiny of the Indian troops, long threatened, finally erupted in 1857 and the whole continent was soon in a ferment. The Betting Book of the 78th has another significant entry: '27th December 1856: Poona: Captain Hunt bets Captain Bogle one bottle of champagne that neither he nor Captain Bogle will be killed in action this time twelvemonth. (Captain Hunt and Captain Bogle both killed.)'

The 78th was engaged in a brief and successful campaign in Persia lasting only a few months after which they returned to India in May 1857 in time to hear the alarming news of the Mutiny and find southern India up in arms. Under General Havelock they formed part of a small force of around 1,000 Europeans, which in July 1857 marched to take Futtegahr and Cawnpore. In each they found the recently murdered and mutilated corpses of English women and children. Grimly, the small force continued fighting and marching until they reached Lucknow in September, the 78th having suffered 122 casualties and won five Victoria Crosses in the process. Here it was clear that they were not strong enough to evacuate the garrison, and over a thousand women and children safely, so they remained as reinforcements.

In the same month, September 1857, the 42nd and 93rd landed at Calcutta where they met their old chief Sir Colin Campbell, recalled from retirement as Commander-in-Chief in India, and greeted him with rapturous cheers. They were to be followed soon by their old comrades the 79th, but meanwhile the 42nd and 93rd together had to make an immediate forced march to the relief of Cawnpore. They covered 78 miles in 36 hours in a heat of 110 degrees. Then the British force of 5,000 faced 25,000 mutineers, but inevitably discipline and experience triumphed.

In February 1858, after some hard fighting, the 42nd and 93rd, joined now by the 79th, went on to the relief of Lucknow. It took them over a fortnight to force their way through the city to the Residency. Storming the Barracks and the Sikanderbagh was but one of the seemingly impossible tasks they performed in the process. As soon as the cannon had battered a small breach in the walls Sir Colin ordered a drummer boy of the 93rd to sound the advance and the entire British force rose as one, rushing with a yell at the wall: 'It was not a cheer, but a concentrated yell of rage and ferocity that made the echoes ring again. Pipe Major MacLeod with seven pipers . . . struck up the Highland charge "The Haughs of Cromdale" also known as "On wi' the Tartan".'

The starving garrison in the Residency had already heard the pipes and knew help was at hand. When the Shah Najaf was captured, the night after the fall of the Sikanderbagh, Sir Colin ordered the 93rd to display their colours from the topmost minaret to show the garrison how far the relieving force had reached. The following morning Lieutenant MacBean, Sergeant Hutchison and Drummer Ross, aged twelve, mounted the topmost minaret to do so, attracting a good deal of fire in the process. Defiantly Drummer Ross played 'Cock of the North' and waved his bonnet. Soon afterwards the Residency was relieved at the points of the Highlanders' bayonets and the garrison, women and children, skilfully evacuated without loss. In the process the 42nd Highlanders had won eight V.C.s and the 93rd Highlanders seven V.C.s.

Following the relief and evacuation of Lucknow the old Highland Brigade was together again. On May 5th, 1858 in the advance on Bareilly they were involved in what Sir Colin Campbell himself described as 'the most determined effort he had seen during the war,' when they were attacked by a large body of Ghazis, or Mussulman fanatics. 'Colonel Cameron of the 42nd was dragged from his horse and would certainly have been slain, but for ... Sergeant Gardiner, who bayoneted two of the fanatics and won ... the Victoria Cross.'

In January 1859 Captain Lawson and 37 men of the 42nd were guarding a river crossing when they were attacked at dawn by a force of 2,000 rebels. Captain Lawson was seriously wounded and his sergeant and other N.C.O.s killed very early in the engagement, but Privates Walter Cook and Duncan Miller took command. They held the enemy at bay from sunrise to sunset and finally drove them back over the river. For this the two Black Watch privates received well-earned V.C.s., and the pipe tune 'Lawson's Men' was composed to commemorate their stand.

By then the mutiny was all but over, although considerable mopping-up operations remained to be done. In these the 92nd, or Gordon Highlanders, and the 71st, or Highland Light Infantry, who had both arrived too late for the real fighting, played their part. It was a frustrating business hunting the rebels, with little satisfaction involved in it and plenty of danger.

The 72nd Duke of Albany's Own Highlanders formed part of Sir Hugh Rose's force in Central India. In the attack on Kotah, Lieutenant Aylmer Cameron won the V.C.

On one occasion the 92nd managed to close on an elusive rebel force, which promptly turned and fled. Lieutenant and Adjutant Humfrey rode ahead of the regiment and attacked one of the rebel leaders. Missing him with his revolver, he threw the empty weapon at the man's head and reached for his claymore, only to find that it had been jerked out of its scabbard during his headlong advance and he was unarmed. The man slashed at Humfrey with his sword and he parried it with his arm. He then jumped off his horse, ducked under its belly, seized his opponent by the leg, hauled him off his horse and dragged him to the ground. When some men of his regiment rushed up to his assistance they found him sitting on his prostrate foe beating his skull on a boulder until he was dead.

Opportunities for distinction of this kind were rare. In the main, the policing operations were a dull job, with the ever present possibility of a sniper's bullet in the back and a nameless grave in some frontier gorge, or isolated outpost, or of a slower, more painful death from cholera, malaria, or some obscure tropical disease. It was a continuous and thankless task with only the rumours of war or rebellion to break the monotony. The next major outbreak came, seventeen years later, with the first Afghan War, when once again the Highlanders distinguished themselves. Both before and afterwards they kept the peace impartially, despite the climate, disease and hostile tribesmen. India was, too often, both their graveyard and their monument.

Chapter 16

In Europe, Spain and Portugal

The behaviour of the Highlanders at Fontenoy has been mentioned already. During the Napoleonic Wars the Highlanders, in common with most British troops, had few opportunities of fighting in Europe, until the later stages. In 1799, however, the 92nd, or Gordon Highlanders, embarked for Holland and fought a bloody battle at Egmont-op-Zee amid the sand dunes, opposing 6,000 Frenchmen with the bayonet and suffering a total of 328 casualties. The entire affair can perhaps be best summed up in the words of a Highlander, who was asked afterwards what it had been like. He replied:

'Ilka lad shot a shentleman to herself.'

The Highlanders again exercised their stalking abilities as one incident showed. Private Ewen Macmillan, foster-brother to Captain Cameron, his company commander, was irritated by the French riflemen firing at them on out-post duty from ranges beyond that of their familiar smooth bore musket, Brown Bess. Seeing one of the French take cover in a position where he felt he could get within range unseen, Macmillan left his post without permission and stalked the rifleman. When he was sure he was within range he raised his musket for a shot, but the Frenchman was too quick for him and fired first, nicking the lobe of his ear. Macmillan fired in reply, wounding his adversary, then rushed in and bayoneted him before he had time to reload. Doubling back to the outpost he pointed to his bleeding ear in aggrieved tones and cried in Gaelic:

'Look what the devil's son did to me.'

'You richly deserved it for leaving your post, Ewen,' replied his captain and foster-brother, reprovingly.

'Ah well, he won't do it again, whatever,' remarked Ewen philosophically as he returned to his position.

Regardless of how the Highlanders had acquitted themselves, the expedition to Holland, as a whole, was a failure. There was an armistice and an exchange of prisoners before the British withdrew to England. The British might defeat the French in other parts of the world, but thereafter the way to final victory in Europe lay through Portugal and Spain and over the Pyrenees.

In May 1808 the Spanish rose against their French conquerors and were joined by the Portuguese. Wellesley, not yet the Duke of Wellington, was sent to their aid. He defeated Marshal Junot at the battle of Vimeiro, when Piper George Clarke of the 71st, badly wounded, distinguished himself by playing them into action. After the ensuing Treaty of Cintra the French withdrew from Portugal and Wellesley was summoned home to explain what seemed over-favourable terms. General Sir John Moore was put in charge of the ill-fated expedition into Spain, which ended with the retreat to Corunna. The 42nd, 92nd, 71st, 91st and 79th Highlanders were all present; the first three particularly distinguishing themselves.

The retreat to Corunna was a dispiriting experience, even if the Highlanders again acquitted themselves well, but it all started quite promisingly. Ensign Hector Innes of the 92nd wrote from Potalegre in Portugal on October 24th, 1808:

> We passed through some of the principal towns in Portugal. They seem at present pretty miserable; war is the ruin of a country . . . We are billeted on the natives, who are very civil, and we live like the sons of kings, but I am sorry to say not very economically; however time passes agreeably . . . I rise at seven, breakfast at nine, read, or walk about the town, dine

at mess at three, parade at five, and since we came we have for the most part passed our evenings at the Convent of St. Barnardo, one of the richest in Portugal. Our music goes down and we spend the night in dancing; in the convent there are several ladies for their education; I believe they are the finest women I ever saw. There seems to be much trade with Ireland and we have eaten Irish butter mostly since we landed.

This leisurely, pleasant existence did not last long. General Sir John Moore, having advanced into Spain, was soon forced to retreat before the converging French armies commanded by Soult on the one side and Napoleon on the other. The notorious winter retreat to Corunna had begun amid freezing mud and slush and appalling weather conditions. Under the strain the British army began to show every sign of disintegrating morale. The one thing that raised the Highlanders' spirits was when they were allowed to turn and fight.

Sergeant Duncan Robertson of the 92nd, describing a small rearguard action, particularly mentions this point:

Everyone was happy that we had got the French in line as we longed very much to fight and abhorred the thought of running away, as we had been doing for some time past. About ten o'clock next morning as the rain was beginning to fall, the French extended their line and beat the charge. They occupied a ploughed field and we were posted on a heath, a small river running between us in the hollow. A farmhouse lay at the foot of the rising ground, having a few stacks of corn about it. The company to which I belonged were ordered to take possession of it and General Hope accompanied us. While moving down, the French fired one of their cannon, the ball falling close beside us, when the general good humouredly took off his hat and saluted the gunner; as there was only one subaltern with the company I got command of a section. When we came to the house we found a part of the French there before us, and a strong reinforcement coming to their assistance. However, they did not think fit to wait and receive us, and, after a few rounds on both sides, they fell back and we occupied the farm, but were not allowed to remain in quiet possession; as the enemy came upon us in overwhelming numbers, we fell back the breadth of the field and posted ourselves behind a stone wall, from whence we opened fire. The French attempted to charge us, but were driven back. On our left was a cart road between two high hedges, and while the party in front were keeping us in play, about forty went up this road, while those in front made a feint of retiring so as to decoy us between two fires. I happened to look round, hoping for help, when I saw the other party forming at the head of the field, not fifty yards from us. It struck me at once to get into line and cut them off from their own line; my section jumped into the road, formed, and prepared to charge; when they saw this they ran down on us; we gave them a volley and eighteen fell killed and wounded. On seeing the fate of their comrades, twenty-two laid down their arms and were taken prisoners. Another detachment came to the rescue and the sergeant commanding it got hold of one of our men, when I leaped back and drove my pike through his body; the others ran off. We were now thoroughly drenched with rain, and when the night came we were relieved by an equal proportion of the regiment. A number of apples were found in the farmhouse, which were greedily devoured. In the evening we got our beef served out, but having neither bread, nor salt, it made an unsavoury supper. Although the weather was cold we slept very comfortably beside large fires we had kindled in the open air.

From Ensign Hector Innes we have an eyewitness account of some of the Gordon's part in the battle of Corunna on January 11th, 1809, when he was on picket duty with his company:

Our sentries were close to the French. Colonel Napier sent me to General Hope, distant about two miles, to inform him of the local situation of our position, distant about three miles from our regiment and brigade. I went accoutred with my trusty claymore and pistol, with my stockings all down. I had to pass quite close to the enemy and through a turnip field, which annoyed me a great deal more. When I returned, I found they had not attacked us. So Tulloch (his cousin in another regiment) and I sat down and ate some cold beef as salt as Lot's wife, but we were soon roused from our meal by some shots which fell at our side, and my servant, who had brought the dinner, was mortally wounded. The business began in about half an hour, when the enemy rushed down instantaneously in crowds in all directions, firing smartly on the pickets (ours on the left). For a while we withstood vigorously their attacks. However, being overpowered by numbers, we retired with loss, and afterwards rallied and took post behind a hedge. I do assure you we had some fun; you would have laughed if you had seen how we scampered with Jack Frenchman at our heels; but fortune favoured us. I commanded a few but trusty men, who after three hours were successful. We charged through the village along with two companies of the 14th Regiment, who, I am rather piqued to find, get all the merit. We certainly gave them a complete thrashing. I had the curiosity to examine the enemy's position and was struck with astonishment to see the awful carnage; they were lying actually all above one another.

A private of the Black Watch wrote:

The Commanding Officer said '42nd Charge'. In one moment every man was up with a cheer, and the sound of his musket and every shot did execution. They were so close upon us that we gave them the bayonet the instant we fired. The confusion that now ensued baffles all my powers, even of memory and imagination—pell-mell, ding-dong—ilka man gat his birdie and many of us skivered pairs, front and rear rank; to the right about they went and we after them. I think I see the grizzly fellows now, running and jumping, as the Highlanders, laughing and swearing and foaming, stuck the pointed steel into their loins. We followed them down the valley and stopped not for General or Commanding Officer. But still on, in the rage and wrath of the Highlander.

A more succinct account ran simply:

> The battle of Corunna was bloody and bravely contested. The French got the devil of a drubbing, though five to one. As they were beat back they always pressed forward with fresh troops. Night put an end to the action.

In the moment of victory General Sir John Moore was killed, but despite the victory and despite being safely evacuated the British Army was in a bad way. Later on, General Sir Colin Campbell would recall how he had been forced to march barefoot in the snow because the soles of his boots had worn completely away, the leather of the uppers being stuck to the flesh. On board ship he only managed to remove them by soaking his feet in hot water and cutting the leather away in strips with his flesh adhering to them in patches.

Captain Seton of the 92nd wrote, on their arrival at Portsmouth on January 25th:

> A passage most dreadful. We are strange figures, all dirty and most of us almost naked. I had not a change of clothes since I was at Lugo on the 5th until last evening, when I bought a shirt and some other things. Our men are in a dreadful state.

According to Sergeant Robertson:

> When we landed at Portsmouth I had neither shoes nor stockings, but had to walk along the streets barefooted; the condition we were in with regard to clothing and cleanliness beggars description; When we came to our billets about six miles from Portsmouth, the inhabitants would not allow us to sleep in their beds, nor sit by their fireside, on account of the vermin that infested us; cleaning ourselves was out of the question. When we reached Weeley Barracks (Colchester) where our heavy baggage was lying, I got a suit of clothes I had

left, and soon divested myself of my filthy raiment and reduced it to ashes, with the exception of the Highland bonnet and feathers.

Sergeant Robertson does not mention the typhus which ran through the army and took its toll from the Highland regiments. However they were again ready in the summer to take part in yet another disastrously conceived expedition this time against the island of Walcheren in Holland. The indecisive Earl of Chatham was in command, which gave rise to the famous rhyme:

'The Earl of Chatham, with sword drawn,
Stood waiting for Sir Richard Strachan.
Sir Richard, longing to be at 'em,
Stood waiting for the Earl of Chatham.'

Walcheren fever, or malaria, attacked the Highlanders. The Black Watch were reduced from 754 to 204 fit men, over five hundred men of the Gordons were laid low, two hundred and eighteen men of the 91st died, the 71st, not quite so badly affected, lost sixty-nine to the fever and maintained that their comparative immunity was due to drinking a medicine composed of brandy and gunpowder. Of the entire British force of 40,000, it was computed that 35,000 were affected.

Wellesley, now Lord Wellington, was back in Portugal and was building the lines of Torres Vedras, behind which he conducted the successful defence of Lisbon. The 71st, or Macleod's Highlanders, and the 79th, or Cameron Highlanders, were the first into action at Fuentes d'Onor on May 3rd 1811. A desperate struggle raged in the village, and the streets were so blocked with bodies it became hard to move in them. Finally, the 74th arrived as reinforcements and the victory went to the Highlanders and the British forces.

Badajos, Arroyo Molinos, Almaraz, Salamanca, the names of the Peninsular battles sound a roll of honour for the Highland regiments. The heat of summer and the rain and mists of winter came and went and whatever the weather conditions, whatever the countryside they fought over, whatever the odds against them, the Highlanders acquitted themselves honourably. The Peninsular campaign was a continuous hard slogging match in which they proved themselves, time after time, the masters of the French.

There was a pleasant surprise for the 92nd on New Year's Day, 1812. They started the day with an attack on the French holding the town of Almandralejo. There was a thick mist in the early hours, then the rain poured down in bucketfuls. The French evacuated the town hastily without awaiting battle. General Hill then posted strong picquets on all the roads leading into it, and marched the rest of his troops into billets in the town. On taking possession of their quarters many of them found savoury stews still on the fires left behind by the French. The wine of the country mixed with their rum and the stews mixed with their rations provided a better end to the New Year's Day than they had anticipated.

On the 5th of January 1812 General Hill retired to Merida where the troops arrived 'looking as if they had been six months in the field instead of ten days'. They had to march through thick adhesive clay, which tore their gaiters to pieces and often wrenched off their shoes, forcing them to march in their hose. After the excellent hospitality he had enjoyed in Almandralejo a private of the 92nd found himself unable to keep up with the regiment. At one of the halts he fell out unnoticed and was fast asleep before the march was resumed.

He woke up in darkness that evening with the fumes of alcohol still clouding his brain, but aware of the enormity of the offence he had committed. He realized that he was liable to be accused of desertion. Throughout the night he conjured up visions of being caught, court-martialled and shot. Finally, at dawn he started to follow the route the regiment had taken, full of dread as to his future.

Afraid to re-join the regiment in daylight he made his way to a village about three miles from headquarters on the opposite bank of the River Guadiana. Here the inhabitants told him of two stragglers from a French column concealed in the village. At once the idea struck him that if he returned with them as prisoners his own transgressions might be overlooked. With the enthusiastic help of the villagers he soon had them captured, with their hands bound behind them, and marched them triumphantly towards his regiment.

Unfortunately an officer of the 92nd met the trio on the bridge over the river, coming from the direction where no troops should have been. He demanded an explanation and the overwrought soldier burst into tears unable to say a word. At length he collected himself and the truth emerged. Fortunately for him, as he had hoped, the two prisoners were accepted as atonement for his lapse.

There was yet another instance of a Highlander using his bonnet as a decoy. At the defence of Alba de Tormes on the 10th of November, 1812 Private Norman Stewart, of the Gordon Highlanders, an excellent shot, became a little separated from others of his regiment opposed to the French skirmishers. He placed his bonnet carefully on a stone to look as if he was lying down behind it and then retreated with his favourite Brown Bess musket, which he called his 'wife', to a position covering all likely approaches. Whenever a Frenchman advanced he was heard to mutter in Gaelic:

'By God, if you'll no halt, you'll get a kiss from my wife.'

In this way he accounted for a considerable number and after the French finally withdrew he returned to pick up his bonnet. It had been shot at so often that it was by then a hopeless wreck and when he tried it on there was a good deal of laughter. Colonel Cameron, the commanding officer, arrived at this point and began to lecture him for carelessness, but learning the background readily forgave him and promised him a new bonnet:

'Aye, or two if you want them.'

Such moments of light relief were to be cherished, for there were few enough of them. Even after the battle of Vittoria in 1813 opened up the way to the Pyrenees, it was hard fighting. At the battle of the Pass of Maya 2,600 British troops held back 11,000 French and the Gordon Highlanders, especially, had heavy casualties. Typical of the grimness with which they fought was the action of William Bisset, a private in the Gordons. Wounded in the thigh, he hobbled away from the action, leaning on his musket with blood flowing copiously from his wound. Halting at a little distance and seeing his comrades still fighting against considerable odds, he returned to his place in the ranks.

'You had better get back and have that wound bandaged,' his officer advised him.

'I must just have another shot at the rascals, sir, before I leave you,' replied Private Bissett.

He had his shot and was reloading to have another when a musket ball broke his arm. This finally forced him to leave the field. Many were not so fortunate. As his comrades fell back at last it was the heaps of dead and dying that held up the advancing enemy.

With the battle of Vittoria in 1813, when Piper MacLaughlan played the 74th to victory as he lay dying, the Highlanders saw the French finally driven into the Pyrenees. Continuous hard fighting steadily forced them back throughout the last months of 1813, culminating in the battles of Nivelle and Nive. Then, during the worst weather in December and January, the army briefly withdrew into winter quarters.

In the words of a Black Watch sergeant:

> With torn shoes and lacerated feet we advanced on the 11th of November under a heavy fall of hail and snow ... Night brought us to a wood, which afforded a little shelter and plenty of fuel for our fires, where until morning we stretched ourselves

round the welcome blaze. On the 12th we continued our march, though slowly, being delayed by frequent halts occasioned by the obstacles thrown in the way of our advance by the enemy ... The smaller streams were now swollen to rivers and all the fields were completely swamped, yet we had to encamp and fortunate were they who found shelter under canvas.

In the vicinity of the camp was an eminence thickly covered with tall furze bushes and under the inviting shade of these our married people found a tolerable shelter by clearing round the bottom and inclining the tops inwardly so as to form an arch, over which a blanket was spread and thus formed a hut with little labour and no expense ... After remaining three days in this place which we termed 'the wet camp' the whole army were ordered into cantonments ...

We were paying at this time two shillings and sixpence for a loaf of bread between two and three pounds weight ... the same price was asked for a pound of brown sugar; a pound of soap was the same price; and an English pint of milk was tenpence, but that could rarely be obtained. Coffee and tea were scarce articles and beyond the reach of a soldier's purse. We toasted the biscuit to serve as a substitute for coffee, and when a little wheat could be obtained it was preferred; we also considered that a very good substitute mess, when boiled in water and left a few minutes to cool and swell ...

In February 1814 the fighting began again more fiercely than ever, as the French fought desperately to preserve their homeland from invasion. The battle of Orthes gained the Highland regiments fresh battle honours and finally the war, and the campaign climaxed in the battle of Toulouse in April. Perversely, neither Soult nor Wellington was aware that Napoleon had already abdicated and that the war was ended, hence thousands of lives, including those of many Highlanders, were unnecessarily thrown away.

The Highland Brigade, consisting of the 42nd, the 79th and the 91st, commanded by Sir Denis Pack, was in the forefront of the assault. The 42nd led the attack over three hundred yards of ploughed fields into the well fortified redoubts:

> In a minute every obstacle was surmounted; the enemy fled as we leaped over the trenches and mounds like a pack of noisy hounds in pursuit, frightening them more by our wild hurrahs than actually hurting them by ball and bayonet,

wrote a Black Watch lieutenant. Of the 500 Highlanders of the Black Watch, scarcely 90 reached the redoubts and of these less than 60 were unwounded, but they carried them regardless. A French officer, who watched them advance unflinchingly into the heavy fire poured down on them, was forced to exclaim in unwilling admiration:

'My God, how firm those *sans culottes* are!'

The 79th, or Cameron Highlanders, and the 91st, or Argyleshire Highlanders, supported them closely, rallying to the attack whenever they were thrown back. All distinguished themselves and suffered heavy casualties. So too did the 74th in the 3rd Division under General Picton. Lieutenant-Colonel Sir George Napier of the 71st, who were only lightly engaged, gave an eyewitness account of the battle:

> This attack was twice renewed and twice were our gallant fellows forced to retire, when, being got into order again, and under tremendous fire of all arms from the enemy, they once more marched onwards, determined to do or die (for they were nearly all Scotch); and having gained the summit of the position, they charged with the bayonet and in spite of every effort of the enemy, drove all before them . . . taking every work at the point of the bayonet. One judgement was that: It was a cluster of Scottish regiments which by mere invincibility and all enduring valour saved Wellington from failure in that great fight.

Apart from a further brief action at Bayonne, this ended the war in Europe. The battalions returned home. Some were disbanded and some were preparing to embark for America. Yet others were in Ireland. Fortunately the majority were still in being when the news arrived in March that Napoleon had escaped from Elba and had already been received with acclaim in Paris. The final battles of Quatre Bras and Waterloo still lay ahead, but sufficient Highland regiments were available to sway the balance yet again.

Let a Black Watch survivor of Quatre Bras and Waterloo describe the halcyon days that followed:

> On the 4th of July we encamped on the right bank of the Seine at Clichy, near Paris, and for ten weeks the produce of the gardens, vineyards, orchards and fields were free to our hands; but this freedom being abused, was withdrawn, yet not until little remained for use; and by that time public confidence was so far restored that our camp was well supplied with every necessary of life; our pay was regular and our rations good . . . Twelve weeks passed pleasantly in this delightful place. October was approaching with its cloudy sky and the trodden fields presented their bleak, neglected appearance, when we struck camp and proceeded to winter-quarters.

It was not long before they returned home across the Channel once more, secure in the knowledge that Napoleon was safely confined in St. Helena and that the peace of Europe was assured. It was nearly a hundred years before Europe was to see kilted troops in action again. By that time, although still '*sans culottes*', there were few real Highlanders left among them, but the spirit of their Highland predecessors, their courage and discipline, remained a cherished tradition, preserved with pride and upheld with honour.

Appendix A

The Cardwell Reforms and their Effects on the Highland Regiments

Mr. Edward Cardwell, later Viscount Cardwell, Secretary of State of War in 1868 in Gladstone's government, a notable reformer and administrator, initiated the much needed modernization of the British Army with a number of sweeping changes, which included the abolition of the purchase of commissions, the institution of the short service system and the army reserve, also the dropping of the old numerals and the merging of regiments into two battalion regiments by coupling the old single battalion regiments, at the same time strictly delineating recruiting areas for each regiment with which they would henceforth be associated. The theory was that one battalion of each regiment should serve abroad, while the second battalion served at home and vice versa, although this seldom worked in practice. These changes took effect by Royal Warrant in 1881.

The Highland regiments were affected as follows: the 42nd, or Royal Highland Regiment, the Black Watch, and the 73rd, its old 2nd Battalion, were joined once more as 1st and 2nd Battalions of the Royal Highland Regiment, the Black Watch. Their recruiting areas were to be the counties of Fife, Forfar and Perth, four-fifths of which were situated in the Lowlands. Their headquarters were to be in Perth.

The 72nd, or Duke of Albany's Own Highlanders, became the 1st Battalion of the Seaforth Highlanders. The 78th Highlanders, or Ross-shire Buffs, became the 2nd Battalion.

Their recruiting area was entirely Highland, including Ross-shire, Sutherland, Caithness, Moray and Nairn. Their headquarters were at Fort George.

The 75th, known as the Stirlingshire Regiment, and the 92nd, or Gordon Highlanders, were also merged. The 75th, which had not worn the kilt since 1809 and had little in common with the 92nd, became the 1st Battalion of the Gordon Highlanders and the 92nd became the 2nd Battalion. A large part of their recruiting area was Lowland and their headquarters were in Aberdeen.

The 91st, Princess Louise's Argyllshire Highlanders, now became the 1st Battalion and the 93rd, or Sutherland Highlanders, the 2nd Battalion of the Argyll and Sutherland Highlanders. Their recruiting area included Argyllshire, but otherwise was entirely Lowland with no connection whatever with Sutherland. Their headquarters were in Stirling.

The only regiment to escape amalgamation under this scheme and to remain a single battalion regiment was the 79th, or Cameron Highlanders, who became the Queen's Own Cameron Highlanders and retained their old tartan. Their recruiting area was Inverness-shire and their headquarters were to be in Inverness, though temporarily at Fort George. Although thus the most truly Highland of the Highland regiments, even they retained few Gaelic speakers.

The 71st Highland Light Infantry and the 74th Highlanders became the 1st and 2nd Battalions, the Highland Light Infantry. Their recruiting area was entirely Lowland and when offered the choice of wearing the kilt or trews, they chose the latter as more suitable for light infantry, unaware at the time that the Lowland infantry regiments would also wear the trews. Their headquarters were in Glasgow and they became in every sense Glasgow's Own. As many evicted Highlanders had swelled Glasgow's population, it might well be that in some ways they ended up the most genuinely Highland of all the erstwhile Highland regiments.

Prior to the Cardwell Reforms it had been obvious, for some time, to those who knew and understood the matter, that the only way to preserve the Highland identity of the Highland regiments was to amalgamate them into one, or at the most two battalions, which would at least be Gaelic speaking and truly Highland. The Government, however, was swayed by the then quite astonishing reactions of the 'perfervid Scots exiles' living in London who at the threat of amalgamations arranged protest marches with pipes and banners and raised country-wide petitions to preserve the identity of the separate regiments. Cardwell, an Englishman, educated at Oxford, could not be expected to understand the intricacies of the Highland relationships. He should at least have consulted the Colonels of the Highland regiments themselves. Only one, the Colonel of the 42nd, was even approached on the subject.

In the event the Cardwell Reforms fell between half a dozen stools and ensured that the truly Highland identity of the Highland regiments would inevitably be lost, finally and for all time. They thus completed, wittingly or unwittingly, the plans Whitehall had advanced in the earliest days of the Highland regiments after the 1745 Rebellion. They ensured that the few Highlanders left in the Highlands could have no entirely Highland regiment to join. The Lowlanders had finally triumphed, but on the other hand, as already shown, the Highlanders in their regiments, in their kilts and tartans, in their clan spirit, their pipe music and their traditional courage and discipline, left a legacy to which the whole of Scotland and indeed the whole of Britain became, in time, proud heir.

Appendix B

The Highland Regiments

1. The 42nd Royal Highland Regiment, or Black Watch. 1740–
Six independent companies of Highlanders raised in 1729 were known as the Black Watch. In 1740 embodied into a regiment under the number 43rd, afterwards changed to 42nd. Became the Royal Highlanders in 1758. In 1881 dropped numeral and became 1st Battalion the Black Watch.
2. Loudon's Highlanders. 1745–1748.
Raised to fight on the continent. Fought at Culloden on Government side. Embarked for Flanders and fought at Bergen-op-Zoom. Were reduced in 1748.
3. Montgomerie's Highlanders or 77th. 1757–1763.
Raised for War in America. Also served in Martinique and Havannah. At the end of war offered land in America. On outbreak of War of Independence those who had chosen land joined Emigrant Highlanders.
4. Fraser's Highlanders or old 78th and 71st Regiments:
78th Regiment, or Fraser's Highlanders. 1757–1763.
Raised to fight in America. At Louisburg and Quebec with Wolfe. Offered the opportunity of staying with a grant of land many of the regiment did so when it was reduced in 1763. In 1775 most of these joined the 84th Royal Highland Emigrants.
71st Highlanders, or Fraser's Highlanders. 1775–1783.
Raised for service in America during the War of Independence. Served at Brooklyn and Savannah, and York River. Reduced in 1783.

5. Keith's and Campbell's Highlanders: 1759–1763.
The old 87th and 88th Highland Regiments.
Raised to fight on the Continent in the Seven Years War. Greatly distinguished themselves in Germany. Reduced at the end of the war in 1763.
6. 89th, or Gordon Highlanders: 1759–1765.
Raised for service in India against the French. Served with remarkable discipline. Not a man brought to halberts. Returned home and reduced in 1765.
7. 101st, or Johnstone's Highlanders. 1760–1763.
Formed to reinforce Keith's and Campbell's Highlanders in Germany. First draft duly did so, but a second draft was not required and both were reduced in 1763 at the end of the Seven Years War.
8. 71st Highland Light Infantry, formed as 73rd, or Lord Macleod's Highlanders: 1777–1881.
Two battalions formed in 1777. 1st Battalion to India. 2nd to Gibraltar, during siege, reduced in 1783. In 1786 1st Battalion renumbered 71st. Service in India, S. Africa, S. America, Peninsula, Waterloo, N. America, Crimea. In 1881 linked with 74th as 1st Battalion Highland Light Infantry.
9. Argyll Highlanders, or old 74th Highland Regiment: 1777–1783.
Raised for War of Independence in N. America. Sailed in 1778 for Halifax, Nova Scotia. Stationed there throughout the war. In action at Penobscot. Reduced 1783.
10. Macdonald's Highlanders, or old 76th Highland Regiment: 1777–1784.
Raised between 1777 and 1784 by Lord Macdonald. Mutinied at Burnt Island. Fought in Virginia, but taken prisoner on Lord Cornwallis's surrender. No case of desertion while prisoners. Returned to Scotland and reduced in 1784.
11. Athole Highlanders, or old 77th Highland Regiment: 1778–1783.

Raised to serve for three years, or duration of war. Served in Ireland, then marched to Portsmouth to be sent to India at the end of war (of Independence). Mutinied. Disbanded in 1783.

12. The 72nd, or Duke of Albany's Own Highlanders, formed as the 78th, or Lord Seaforth's Highlanders: 1778–1881.
Mutinied at Leith prior to embarkation for India. Badly affected by journey. Gave up kilt 1809. Trews worn 1823. In 1881 became 1st Battalion of the Seaforth Highlanders, (Ross-shire Buffs) the 78th Highlanders becoming the 2nd Battalion. Returned to kilt.

13. The Aberdeenshire Highland Regiment, or old 81st Highland Regiment: 1777–1783.
Raised in 1777 and stationed in Ireland. In 1783 about to be embarked for East Indies, contrary to terms of engagement. On hearing of mutiny of Athole Highlanders they refused to go. The Government then disbanded them in Edinburgh in 1783.

14. The Royal Highland Emigrant Regiment, or old 84th Highland Regiment: 1775–1783.
This battalion was to be raised in 1775 from the Highland emigrants in Canada, the discharged men of the 42nd and Fraser's and Montgomerie's Highlanders, who had settled in N. America after the peace of 1763. Defended Quebec. A 2nd Battalion was formed. Both were reduced in 1783.

15. The 42nd, or Royal Highland Regiment, 2nd Battalion, also known as the 73rd Regiment. 1780–
Raised in 1780 as the 2nd Battalion of the 42nd. Stationed in India. Became 73rd in 1784, after the siege of Mangalore. In 1809 ceased to be Highland. In 1873 was linked with the 90th. In 1881 reverted to 2nd Battalion of the Black Watch as a Highland regiment once more.

16. The 74th Highland Regiment of Foot. 1787–1881.

Raised in 1787, embarked for India 1788. At battle of Assaye. Returned Britain 1805. In 1809 ceased to wear the kilt. 1816 ceased to be Highland. In 1845 resumed title Highland. Also resumed wearing trews. In 1881 became the 2nd Battalion of the Highland Light Infantry.

17. The 75th Regiment, or 1st Battalion Gordon Highlanders. 1787–1881.
Raised in 1787 for service in India. Returned Britain 1806. In 1809 ceased to be designated Highland, or to wear the kilt. Until 1881 known as the Stirlingshire Regiment, while retaining its old number. In 1881 became the 1st Battalion Gordon Highlanders and resumed kilt and Highland dress.

18. The 78th Highlanders, or Ross-shire Buffs, or 2nd Battalion Seaforth Highlanders. 1793–1881.
Raised in 1793 by Francis Mackenzie, afterwards Lord Seaforth. A 2nd Battalion was raised in 1794. This was amalgamated in 1796. Another 2nd Battalion was raised in 1804 and amalgamated in 1817. In 1881 became 2nd Battalion Seaforth Highlanders, Duke of Albany's Ross-shire Buffs.

19. The 79th Queen's Own Cameron Highlanders. 1793–
Raised by Alan Cameron of Erracht in 1793. In 1873 made 'Queen's Own'. In 1881 the only Highland regiment unaffected by the Cardwell Reforms. Retained own tartan.

20. The 91st Princess Louise's Argyllshire Highlanders. 1794–1881.
Raised in 1794 by the Duke of Argyll. Originally numbered the 98th. In 1798 the number altered to the 91st. In 1809 changed from kilts to trews. In 1810 reverted to ordinary infantry uniform. In 1864 changed from 91st Foot to 91st Argyllshire Highlanders. Reverted to trews. In 1871 became Princess Louise's Argyllshire Highlanders. In 1881 amalgamated with 93rd as 1st

Battalion of Princess Louise's (Argyll and Sutherland Highlanders.)

21. The 92nd or Gordon Highlanders. 1794–1881.
Raised by the Marquis of Huntly in 1794. In 1861 titled the Gordon Highlanders. In 1881 became the 2nd Battalion of the Gordon Highlanders with the 75th as the 1st Battalion.

22. The 93rd, or Sutherland Highlanders. 1800–1881.
Raised in 1800 by Major-General Wemyss of Wemyss. In 1813 a 2nd Battalion was formed. Sent to Newfoundland. Returned to Britain in 1815 and reduced. 1815 1st Battalion sent to N. America. New Orleans. In 1881 amalgamated with 91st Princess Louise's Argyll Highlanders as 2nd Battalion of Princess Louise's (Argyll and Sutherland Highlanders.)

Other Highland Regiments:

1745–1747. Two battalions of Campbell or Argyll Highlanders were raised in Argyllshire and the West on the Hanoverian side. 1,200 men.
Twenty Companies of 100 each were raised in Inverness and Ross on the Hanoverian side.
Macleod of Macleod raised 200 for the Hanoverian side.
Grant of Grant raised 98 for the Hanoverian side.
Lord George Murray on the Stuart side raised 1,400 men in his brother the Duke of Atholl's country.
All these were reduced by 1749.

1756–1763. During the Seven Years War, independent companies were again enrolled in the Highlands and recruits obtained for new regiments in the south.
100th Regiment of the Line raised by Major Colin Campbell embodied at Stirling in 1761, served in Martinique and reduced in Scotland in 1763.
105th Regiment of the Line (The Queen's Highlanders)

embodied at Perth 1762, served Ireland and reduced 1763. Raised by Colonel David Graeme, two battalions.
Two regiments (113th Regiment Royal Highland Volunteers) raised by Major James Hamilton and Captain Allan Maclean seem to have served as depot battalions for drafts for overseas Highland regiments. Reduced 1763.

1793–1815. The 116th, 132nd and 133rd Regiments of Highlanders were raised but soon afterwards broken up and transferred to other corps.

Appendix C

The Fencible Regiments

Fencible regiments for the internal defence of the country, unlike the Militia, were formed by the ordinary recruiting methods and as in regiments of the line the officers were appointed and their Commissions signed by the King.

During the Seven Years War. 1756–1763:

1. The Argyll Regiment (No 1). Raised 1759. Numbered about 1,000 men. Disbanded in 1763.
2. The Sutherland Regiment (No 1). Raised 1759. Numbered 1,050. Noted for outstanding behaviour. Disbanded 1763.

During the American War of Independence. 1776–1783:

1. The Argyll, or Western Regiment (No 2). Embodied at Glasgow in 1778 and reduced 1783.
2. The Gordon Regiment (No. 1). Raised in 1778 by the Duke of Gordon. Embodied at Aberdeen in 1778 and reduced 1783.
3. The Sutherland Regiment (No. 2). Raised in Sutherland and Caithness in 1779, stationed chiefly near Edinburgh. Disbanded in 1783, but many of the men subsequently joined the 93rd Sutherland Highlanders.

During the European Wars. 1793–1815:

1. The Argyll Regiment (No. 3) ultimately of 3 battalions. First raised by Marquis of Lorne embodied in 1793, reduced 1799. Second raised by Colonel Henry Clavering in 1794 served in Ireland and reduced 1792. Third raised by Colonel Archibald Macneil in 1799, enlisted

for service anywhere in Europe and sent to Gibraltar in 1800 and reduced in 1802.

2. The Breadalbane Regiment. Also of three battalions. Raised by the Earl of Breadalbane. 1st and 2nd Battalions raised at Perth in 1793 and reduced in 1798. The 3rd, raised in 1794, served in Ireland and was disbanded in 1802.
3. The Gordon Regiment (No. 2), or Northern Fencible Highlanders. Embodied at Aberdeen in 1793 and volunteered to serve outside Scotland. Sent to Kent in 1794. Reviewed in London by George III who had never seen a Highland regiment. Only the 2nd Highland regiment reviewed. (42nd in 1743 was the first). Reduced in 1798.
4. The Grant, or Strathspey Regiment, or Fencible Men in North Britain. Raised by Sir James Grant of Grant. Embodied at Forres in 1793. Reduced in 1799.
5. The Sutherland Regiment (No. 3). Raised in Sutherland by General Wemyss of Wemyss. Embodied in 1793. In 1797 extended its service to Ireland and helped suppress Irish Rebellion. Was reduced in 1798, but the men mostly joined the 93rd Sutherland Highlanders in 1800.
6. The Caithness Regiment, or Rothesay and Caithness Regiment, raised by Sir John Sinclair of Ulbster. The first enrolled for service anywhere in Britain. There were two battalions. The 1st was embodied at Inverness in 1794 and reduced at Bruntsfield Links, Edinburgh, in 1799. The 2nd battalion was embodied at Forfar in 1795 and after serving in Ireland volunteered in 1797 for service abroad. It supplied volunteers to the 72nd and 92nd Highland Regiments in 1800, but did not go abroad and was reduced in 1802.
7. The Caithness Legion. Raised by Sir Benjamin Dunbar, in 1794–1796 for service in Ireland. Reduced in 1802.
8. The Dumbarton Regiment. Raised by Colonel Campbell of Stonefield, in 1794. Active in Ireland during the Rebellion. Reduced in 1802.

9. The Fraser Regiment. Raised by James Fraser of Belladrum in 1794. Embodied 1795. Served throughout Irish Rebellion. Reduced in 1802.

10. The Glengarry, or British Highland Regiment. Raised by Alexander Macdonell of Glengarry in 1794, served in Jersey and Guernsey and was reduced in 1802. The greater part of the Glengarry men then emigrated to Canada and settled in the district named after their native Glen. During the American War of 1812–14 they formed along with other emigrants a regiment called the Glengarry Fencibles.

1. The Inverness-shire Regiment, or Loyal Inverness Fencible Highlanders. Raised for service within the British Isles by Major Baillie of Duncan and embodied at Inverness in 1795. Active in suppressing Irish Rebellion and name changed to Duke of York's Royal Inverness-shire Highlanders. Disbanded 1802.

12. The Reay Regiment. Raised by George Mackay of Bighouse in 1794 in the Reay country and embodied at Fort George in 1795. Served in Ireland during the Rebellion. Disbanded in 1802.

13. The Ross-shire Regiment. Embodied in 1796 by Major Colin Mackenzie of Mountgerald. Small in numbers but excellent in behaviour. Not a man punished by the time they were reduced, in 1802.

14. The Clan Alpine Regiment. Raised by Colonel Alexander Macgregor Murray and embodied at Stirling in May 1799, to serve anywhere in Europe. Occupied various stations in Ireland and was reduced in 1802.

15. The Lochaber Regiment. Raised by Cameron of Lochiel and embodied at Falkirk in 1799. Served in Ireland and reduced in 1802.

16. The Regiment of the Isles, or Macdonald's Fencible Regiment, raised by Lord Macdonald on his estates in the Western Isles and embodied in 1799. Served in Lowlands and north of England. Reduced in 1802.

17. The Ross and Cromarty Rangers. Raised by Colonel Lewis Mackenzie in June 1799 for service in any part of Europe. Never left Scotland and reduced in 1802.
18. The Macleod, or Princess Charlotte of Wales' Regiment. Raised by John Macleod of Colbecks in 1799. The last Fencible Regiment formed in the Highlands. Served in Ireland and reduced 1802.

Bibliography

Sketches of the Character, Manners and Present State of the Highlanders of Scotland with Details of the Military Service of The Highland Regiments: by Major General David Stewart of Garth: 2 vols: Edinburgh 1822. Reprinted 1825.

A History of the Scottish Highlands, Clans and Regiments. J. S. Keltie, Edinburgh 1887. 2 vols.

The Life of a Regiment: Colonel Greenhill Gardyne. Edinburgh 1901. 3 vols.

Reminiscences of Military Service with the 93rd Sutherland Highlanders: Surgeon General William Munro. London 1883.

Records of Service and Campaigning in Many Lands: Surgeon General William Munro. 2 vols. London 1887.

Reminiscences of the Great Mutiny: W. Forbes-Mitchell. Late Sergeant 93rd. London 1893.

Am Reismeid Chataich: The 93rd Sutherland Highlanders, or 2nd Bn., The Argyll and Sutherland Highlanders. Brigadier A. E. J. Cavendish. 1928.

Diary: Lt. James Ewart: 93rd. 1811–1815.

Recollections of a Military Life: Sergeant Morris. 73rd.

The Siege of Bangalore: By an Officer Present.

Military Reminiscences. Polygar Campaigns. Colonel Welsh.

Reminiscences of a Campaign. John Malcolm. 42nd. 1839.

Retrospect of a Military Life. Q. M. S. Anton: 42nd. 1841.

Five Years in Kaffirland: Second War: Mrs. Harriet Ward.

A Black Watch Episode of the Year 1731. H. D. MacWilliam. W. & A. K. Johnston. 1908.

Letters from an English Officer in the Highlands to a Friend in London: Captain Burt.

A Military History of Perthshire:

The Black Watch. A. Mackay Scobie: Ms.
Reminiscences and Recollections of Captain Gronow.
Military History: Cannon.
The Black Watch. Bernard Fergusson. 1955. Collins.
Reminiscences of a Soldier. Colonel W. K. Stuart. London 1874.
Life of Sir David Baird. Wilkins. London. 1912.
Life of Sir Colin Campbell. Colonel Shadwell. London 1881.
The Campaign of New Orleans. Rev. G. R. Gleig. London 1836.
The Highland Brigade. James Cromb. Aeneas Mackay. London 1902.
Autobiographical Journal of John Macdonald, Schoolmaster anu Soldier. 1770–1830. Edinburgh 1906.
Annals of the Disruption. Rev. Thomas Brown. 1843.
Cassell's British Battles. James Grant.
Sketches of Sutherland Characters. A. Mackay. Edinburgh 1889.
Memorabilia Domestica: Rev. Donald Sage. Wick 1889.
Gloomy Memories of the Highlands. Donald Macleod. Glasgow 1892.
Superstitions of the Highlanders. Mrs. Grant.
One Hundred Years in the Highlands. Osgood Mackenzie: Bles.
The Highlander in Anecdote and Story. Mackay.
Journal of Lieutenant Ronald Campbell of the Grenadier Company 72nd Regiment. 2 vols.
First Statistical Account of Scotland.
Proud Heritage: Official History of the H.L.I. 4 vols: Colonel L. B. Oatts. 1959.
Famous Regiment Series: Leo Cooper, Ltd. London:
The Argyll and Sutherland Highlanders: Douglas Sutherland.
The Black Watch: Philip Howard.
The Gordon Highlanders: Christopher Sinclair-Stephenson.
The Highland Light Infantry. L. B. Oatts.
Regimental Magazines, Journals, Records, Diaries, etc.
Betting Book of the 2nd Battalion Seaforth Highlanders. etc.
Bibliography of the Legend of Duncan Campbell of Inverawe:
Inverawe and Ticonderoga: A. P. Stanley. Fraser's Magazine: October 1880.
Ticonderoga: A Poem. R. L. Stevenson. Scribner's Magazine. December 1887.
Historical Handbook of the Northern Tour. Appendix G, *Montcalm and Wolfe.* Francis Parkman. Boston 1885.

New York State Historical Proceedings. Vol. II Fort Edward Book. pp. 80–88. Robert O. Bascomb.
Vol. X of the Proceedings of the New York State Historical Association.
The Black Watch at Ticonderoga. F. B. Richards, Glen Falls, New York, Sec. to the N.Y. State Hist. Assn.
Atlantic Monthly. C. F. Gordon Cumming. September 1884.
Lake George and Lake Champlain. W. Max Reid.
Tales of the Highlands. Sir Thomas Dick Lauder.
Winsor's Critical and Narrative History of the United States.
Records of Argyle. Lord Archibald Campbell. W. Blackwood. 1885.
Book of Dreams and Ghosts. Longmans. 1897.
The Magazine of History. July 1906.

INDEX